THE AMERICAN SCENE: EVENTS

Volume 5
Rise to World Power: 1891-1917

GROLIER
EDUCATIONAL

First published in the United States of America in 1999 by Grolier Educational, Sherman Turnpike, Danbury, CT 06816

When citing this publication, use the following wording:
The American Scene: Events, 9 volumes, Danbury, CT: Grolier Educational, 1999.

Project Director: Kenneth W. Leish
Director of Art & Design: Nancy Hamlen
Design: Millward and Millward Graphic Design
Assistant Editor: Maria McAllister
Copy Editor: Meghan Fiero
Photo Researchers: Paula Wehde, Martin Levick
Index: Pauline Sholtys
Manufacturing:
        Vice President: Joseph J. Corlett
        Director, Reference Publications: Christine L. Matta
        Production Manager: Elizabeth C. Steger
        Production Assistant: Susan E. Zaleta

Library of Congress Cataloging-in-Publication Data

The American scene: events.

        p.   cm.

Contents: v. 1. Before independence: to 1775 — v. 2. A new nation emerges: 1776-1828 — v. 3. Growth and conflicts: 1829-1862 — v. 4. Civil War and its aftermath: 1863-1890 — v. 5. Rise to world power: 1891-1917 — v. 6. World War I and the Depression, 1918-1941 — v. 7. World War II and the Cold War: 1942-1958 — v. 8. Superpower: 1959-1982 — v. 9. America today: 1983-
        Includes index.
        ISBN 0-7172-9448-X (set : alk. paper)
        1. United States—History—Juvenile literature. [1. United States—History.] I. Grolier Educational (Firm)
        E178.3.A625 1999   98-44206
        973—dc21   CIP
                                                                    AC

Printed in the United States of America

Contents

Introduction 4

Early Days of Basketball — U.S. Buys the Virgin Islands 5

Set Index 97

Welcome to THE AMERICAN SCENE

The history of the United States is not just a list of dates and names. It is an ongoing adventure, far more exciting than any movie or television show. It is the story of brave men and women who built a great nation from a wilderness. It's the story of bloody battles and dangerous journeys and amazing inventions. It is great achievements in art, literature, and music. It is baseball, and Hula-Hoops, and shiny new automobiles. It is the story of countless triumphs and tragedies. And it is the story of dreams and aspirations, of which many have come true and many are yet to be realized.

Each page in **THE AMERICAN SCENE** tells one small part of our national saga. Information is presented in several different ways:

1. At the top of each page, you'll find a **FACT BOX** that summarizes the information presented about an event, a particular year's occurrences, or some interesting aspect of our history.

2. A large **ILLUSTRATION** brings each event or person to life.

3. A **CAPTION** explains what each illustration shows.

4. A **MAP** shows where each event took place, or how many states there were in the nation in a particular year.

5. To the side of each page, a **TIMELINE** indicates when the event occurred.

6. The **TEXT** describes each event briefly and colorfully.

7. At the end of the text, a section entitled **DID YOU KNOW** presents an interesting fact that you may find surprising.

8. Finally, you'll notice that each page falls within one of nine **COLOR-CODED CATEGORIES**. Each category has its own symbol and color. The nine categories are:

   - **Important Events** (orange): the major happenings in American history
   - **Notable People** (blue): men and women who played key roles in the growth of the United States
   - **Discoveries & Inventions** (dark green): trailblazers in exploration, science, and technology
   - **A Year to Remember** (red): an overview of events and life in America during key years in our history
   - **Arts & Entertainment** (yellow): the great performers, writers, artists, and musicians, and the movies, books, and shows Americans have loved
   - **Famous Places** (turquoise): historic sites that can be visited today
   - **Life in America** (light green): everyday American life through the decades, including sports, fads, fashions, occupations, and holidays
   - **America at War** (purple): the battles and leaders who have made American military history
   - **The Melting Pot** (brown): the many groups whose contributions have made America great

You can look up specific topics by consulting the **SET INDEX** that appears at the end of each volume. Or you can just browse through the books and enjoy the fascinating story of our country's past.

Early Days of Basketball

Early days of basketball

When:
Invented in 1891

Where:
Springfield, Massachusetts

Who:
James A. Naismith

Illustration: The Yale University basketball team of 1901, when the game was just ten years old. (The Granger Collection)

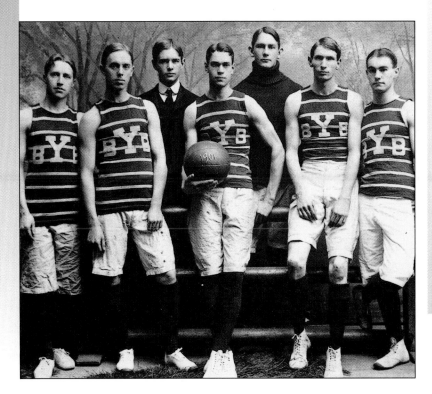

Before slam dunks and alley-oops, there were two peach baskets and a soccer ball. With those baskets and that ball, James Naismith invented one of the world's most popular sports, basketball.

In 1891, Naismith was a young gym instructor at a YMCA training school in Springfield, Massachusetts. During the winter his students got tired of doing gym exercises. The wanted a game to play indoors. So Naismith nailed two peach baskets at either end of the gym 10 feet above the floor. Then, he divided the students into two teams and told them the object of the new game—to throw the ball into the other team's basket.

Within 20 years, basketball was being played across the U.S. The basket did not have a backboard. Players tended to be much shorter than today's stars, and they played slowly. To shoot from a distance they stopped, set, and tossed the ball up with two hands. The one-hand outside shot and the jumper came much later. The first professional teams were made up of working men who liked to play in the evenings. As for Naismith, he became a coach at the University of Kansas, where he taught students to excel at the challenging game he had invented.

Did you know...

Basketball players are sometimes called "cagers" because many early courts were enclosed in a metal or net cage. The ball couldn't go out of bounds!

Before 1750

1750-1799

1800-1849

1850-1899

1900-1924

1925-1949

1950-1974

1975-2000

The Homestead Strike

Important Events

The Homestead strike

What:
A bloody battle between a labor union and big business

Where:
Homestead, Pennsylvania

When:
June 29–November 20, 1892

Illustration: Strikers look down on the Carnegie steelworks at Homestead, Pennsylvania, in 1892. (The Bettmann Archive)

In 1892, in Homestead, Pennsylvania, the struggle between America's industrialists and the men who worked in their factories erupted into violence.

Andrew Carnegie, the owner of the Carnegie Steel Company, believed that the steelworkers were overpaid and inefficient. He decided to break their union, the Amalgamated Association of Iron, Steel, and Tin Workers. With that goal in mind, Carnegie put union buster Henry Clay Frick in charge of his steel mill in Homestead. Frick immediately ordered an increase in production and a cut in wages. When the union struck on June 29, 1892, Frick fired the whole workforce. The outraged workers seized control of the plant and the entire town. Frick then hired "Pinkertons," a private police force that specialized in crushing labor disturbances. Approaching the barricaded river city by barge, the Pinkertons were met by

3,000 strikers, who tossed dynamite at them. A daylong battle followed, leaving nine strikers and seven Pinkertons dead.

On July 12, the governor of Pennsylvania sent in the state militia. Under its protection, Frick imported nonunion labor and resumed production. The broken union held on until November 20, when it officially gave up its strike. Steel became a nonunion industry and remained so until the 1930's.

Did you know...

Henry Frick's New York City mansion and superb art collection are now open to the public.

The Pledge of Allegiance

The Pledge of Allegiance

What:
A pledge of loyalty recited in front of the American flag

When:
Original version published in 1892

Who:
Written by Francis Bellamy

Illustration: Children in a Vermont public school pledge their allegiance to the U.S. flag. (Corbis-Bettmann)

Before 1750

1750-1799

1800-1849

1850-1899

1900-1924

1925-1949

1950-1974

1975-2000

"I pledge allegiance to the flag of the United States of America and to the Republic for which it stands, one Nation under God, indivisible, with liberty and justice for all." Millions of Americans learned those words in school, where each day began with the recitation of the Pledge of Allegiance. The pledge was written more than 100 years ago, as a way to teach American children respect for their flag and their country.

The pledge first appeared in a children's magazine, *The Youth's Companion*, in an issue celebrating the 400th anniversary of Columbus' first voyage to America. Francis Bellamy, the magazine's editor, is considered the primary author of the pledge. In October, 1892, some schoolchildren began reciting the pledge, standing and saluting the flag as they spoke. Soon, schools across America made the pledge part of their daily program.

The pledge became the country's official flag pledge in 1943. But children are no longer required to recite it each day. The U.S. Supreme Court has ruled that forcing children to recite the pledge, or forcing teachers to lead it, violates an important right represented by the flag: freedom of speech.

Did you know...

Bellamy's pledge read: "I pledge allegiance to my flag and to the republic for which it stands, one nation, indivisible, with liberty and justice for all." The present version was adopted in 1954.

Ellis Island

Ellis Island Immigration Museum

What:
The main entry point to America for European immigrants

When:
1892 – 1943

Where:
New York Harbor

Illustration: The Ellis Island Immigration Museum. (© Rafael Macia/Photo Researchers)

For millions of poor and oppressed people, America was the land of freedom and opportunity. The doorway to that promised land was Ellis Island, a small island in New York Bay, within sight of the tall buildings of New York City.

From 1892 to 1943, Ellis Island was the main American immigration center. More than 16 million people, newly arrived from Europe, passed through its warehouse-like buildings. Most of them were poor; all of them wanted a better life for themselves and their children. But first they had to be officially admitted to America. On Ellis Island they were examined by doctors to be sure that they were healthy. They were asked questions about their possessions and about the sponsors who were to meet them. Some were given heartbreaking news; they were sent back to Europe, usually because they were not healthy. But for most,

the dream came true. They were ferried to New York City to begin a new life in America.

Today, four out of ten Americans has an ancestor who arrived at Ellis Island. The government stopped using Ellis Island as its major immigration center in 1943. But Ellis Island was too important to forget. In 1990, it opened as a museum of America's immigration heritage. Today, thousands of visitors come to Ellis Island, this time *from* America.

Did you know...

Ellis Island is named for Samuel Ellis, a New York merchant who once owned the island.

Before 1750

1750-1799

1800-1849

1850-1899

1900-1924

1925-1949

1950-1974

1975-2000

A Year to Remember

1893

President:
Grover Cleveland

States:
44

Major event:
Financial panic grips America

Illustration: A cartoon in magazine showed Uncle Sam shooting the hard times of 1893. (The Granger Collection)

1893

In May, 1893, the stock market crashed, setting off the economic depression known as the "Panic of 1893." More than 15,000 businesses failed, including 600 banks and one-third of the country's railroads. There was massive unemployment. Suddenly, a silver dollar was worth less than 60 cents.

More than 100,000 people decided to try their luck in the Oklahoma Territory. Two years before, the U.S. government had purchased six million acres of Cherokee land in north-central Oklahoma. In 1893, the government offered settlers the chance to claim inexpensive homesteads there. As a result, the largest land rush in history took place on September 16, 1893, when 50,000 settlers claimed land in Oklahoma in a single day.

The nation's economic troubles did not halt the advance of technology. In Detroit, Henry Ford built the first successful gasoline engine and moved one step closer to his dream of creating an automobile. In New Jersey, Thomas Edison constructed a film studio. In Boston, the first long-distance telephone call was made, to New York City. And in Chicago, African-American physician Daniel Hale Williams repaired a stab victim's wounds by performing the world's first open-heart surgery.

Did you know...

Hawaii's Queen Liliuokalani was overthrown in an 1893 revolution engineered by American sugar merchant Sanford Dole.

Before 1750

1750-1799

1800-1849

1850-1899

1900-1924

1925-1949

1950-1974

1975-2000

World's Columbian Exposition

World's Columbian Exposition

What:
An international fair marking the 400th anniversary of Christopher Columbus' first trip to America

Where:
Chicago, Illinois

When:
May 1 to October 30, 1893

Illustration: The World's Columbian Exposition in Chicago in 1893. (The Granger Collection)

The World's Columbian Exposition of 1893 was attended by more than 27 million people. Sometimes called the Chicago World's Fair, it celebrated the 400th anniversary of Christopher Columbus' arrival in America. Gleaming buildings of its "White City" stretched for two miles along the shore of Lake Michigan. At night, they glowed with electric lights, a wondrous sight at that time. Soaring above the buildings was a new invention, a 250-foot-high Ferris Wheel.

The exposition's 150 buildings were designed by the world's top architects. Most of the buildings had white plaster facades, giving rise to the nickname "White City." Inside were the latest technical and artistic marvels, as well as exhibits sponsored by the states and by many countries.

Perhaps the chief wonder of the exposition was electricity, still unfamiliar to many Americans. It powered not only lights, but also the fountains and the rides, including the Ferris Wheel. One popular attraction generated her own electricity. She was Little Egypt, a belly dancer who scandalized the exposition by performing the "hootchy-kootchy."

Did you know...

The Ferris Wheel was designed by George Ferris, a civil engineer. A ride—two long, slow turns of the wheel—lasted 20 minutes.

Before 1750

1750-1799

1800-1849

1850-1899

1900-1924

1925-1949

1950-1974

1975-2000

Discoveries & Inventions

The Burroughs adding machine

What:
The first reliable adding machine

Who:
Invented by William Seward Burroughs

When:
Patented in 1893

Where:
Manufactured in St. Louis, Missouri

The Burroughs Adding Machine

Illustration: The Burroughs adding machine (front right) was welcomed by America's office workers. (Charles Babbage Institute, University of Minnesota)

William Burroughs' father was an unsuccessful inventor who urged his son to choose a more dependable career. Taking his father's advice, Burroughs became a bank clerk. But after dreary hours of adding and re-adding numbers, Burroughs longed for a machine to ease the drudgery of his job. So he decided to invent one.

There were a few adding machines available in the early 1880's, but they were awkward and unreliable. Burroughs began to sketch a mechanical "arithmometer" that would overcome those problems. In 1884, investors gave him $700 to develop his idea. Five years and several prototypes later, he had a hand-cranked machine that seemed to work. He produced 50 of them, but they were a disaster: When operators pulled the crank at different speeds, the machines gave wildly inaccurate results.

Burroughs convinced his backers to fund one more attempt. This time, by devising a mechanism to control the speed of the crank, he assured that the machine would give the same result no matter how the handle was pulled. Consequently, the machines became enormously successful—they were the first adding machines to be widely used in banks and offices.

Did you know...

In 1905, Burroughs founded the Burroughs Adding Machine Company. It is now part of Unisys, a major computer company.

Before 1750

1750-1799

1800-1849

1850-1899

1900-1924

1925-1949

1950-1974

1975-2000

Public Education

Illustration: A one-room schoolhouse in the Midwest during the nineteenth century. (Library of Congress)

Before 1750

1750-1799

1800-1849

1850-1899

1900-1924

1925-1949

1950-1974

1975-2000

In 1647, the colony of Massachusetts passed a law requiring that all towns with more than 50 families provide an elementary school and teacher for its children. That law marked the beginning of public education in America.

Yet not everyone believed that schools should be free and open to all children. Until the middle of the nineteenth century, most American schools were private; many were operated by religious groups. Because some people did not think that tax money should be used to educate poor children, most children attended for only three years. But leaders such as Thomas Jefferson and Daniel Webster fought to establish a system of free, compulsory public education. "Open the doors of the schoolhouse to all the children of the land," Webster said in 1837. Most New England and Midwestern states instituted public education

before the Civil War; the Middle Atlantic and Southern states did not introduce state school systems until later. But by the beginning of the twentieth century, free public schools were available to all children. At that time, schooling was much the same across the country. Children sat at benches or desks and learned reading, writing, and arithmetic. They competed in spelling bees, did sums on blackboards, and read stories that stressed the value of honesty, thrift, and hard work from books called *McGuffey Readers*.

Did you know...

During the nineteenth century, schools in some farm areas were open only 60 days a year.

The Trial of Lizzie Borden

The trial of Lizzie Borden

What:
A sensational murder trial

When:
June 6–21, 1893

Where:
Fall River, Massachusetts

Illustration: Lizzie Borden, who was acquitted of murdering her parents with an ax. (The Granger Collection)

Before 1750

1750-1799

1800-1849

1850-1899

1900-1924

1925-1949

1950-1974

1975-2000

Lizzie Borden took an ax
And gave her mother 40 whacks.
When she saw what she had done,
She gave her father 41.

That familiar rhyme was inspired by a brutal double murder in Fall River, Massachusetts. Lizzie Borden, a 32-year-old Sunday-school teacher, was accused of killing her father and stepmother with an ax.

One day in August, 1892, Borden ran to a neighbor's house, screaming that her parents had been murdered. Their mutilated bodies were found in the family home, but there was no evidence of intruders. At first, Borden said she had been asleep upstairs when the murders occurred. Later, she claimed she had been in the barn and had heard nothing. She was soon arrested for the gruesome killings.

The evidence against Borden was only circumstantial. She was known to dislike her stepmother. Her father was a wealthy man. She had tried to buy poison the day before the murders. And she had burned a stained dress the day after the killings. The defense presented witnesses who told of her good character and her many charitable and religious activities. The jury acquitted Borden of the murders, but many townspeople remained convinced of her guilt. The case was never solved and Borden continued to live in Fall River until her death at the age of 67.

Did you know...

The house where the murders took place is now the "Lizzie Borden Bed & Breakfast."

The Zipper

Before 1750

1750-1799

1800-1849

1850-1899

1900-1924

1925-1949

1950-1974

1975-2000

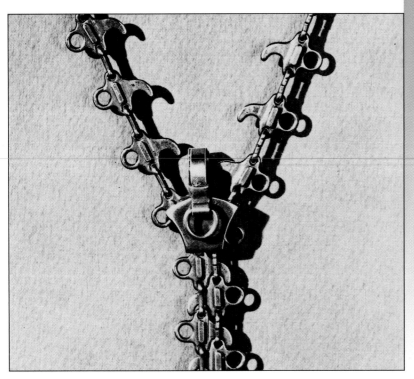

The zipper

What:
A quick way to fasten clothing and other items

When:
Patented in 1893

Who:
Whitcomb L. Judson

Where:
Illinois

Illustration: Judson's slide fastener, forerunner of the modern zipper. (New York Public Library)

Zippers on jackets, zippers on jeans, zippers on suitcases—most Americans use zippers dozens of times every day. Imagine how time-consuming and annoying it would be to use buttons or hooks instead. Yet that's what everyone did before 1893, when Whitcomb L. Judson introduced his slide fastener, the ancestor of the modern zipper.

An Illinois engineer, Judson developed the slide fastener as a quick way to close the fitted boots that were fashionable at the time. Called a clasp locker, his system consisted of a series of hooks and eyes that could be fastened and unfastened with a sliding clasp. It was exhibited at the 1893 World Columbian Exposition in Chicago.

Judson's fastener was an improvement over individual buttons, but it was still cumbersome. So Judson hired Swedish engineer Gideon Sundback to improve it. In 1913, Sundback developed a fastener that, like today's zippers, used interlocking metal teeth instead of hooks and eyes. Eagerly adopted by the public, these new fasteners were in wide use by the 1920's.

Did you know...

The B. F. Goodrich Company used sliding fasteners for its rubber galoshes and introduced the name "zipper" in 1922. The name was inspired by the sound the teeth made when the slide was zipped up and down.

14

"Coxey's Army"

What:
A protest march from Ohio to Washington, D.C., by unemployed workers

When:
1894

Who:
Led by Jacob Coxey, an Ohio businessman

"Coxey's Army"

Illustration: "Coxey's Army" on its way to Washington in 1894. (Brown Brothers)

In 1894, the United States was in the midst of the worst depression it had ever known. Many businesses failed, and thousands of people lost their jobs. Jacob Coxey, an Ohio businessman and reformer, thought he had a solution to the unemployment problem. He wanted the government to create road-building projects to employ the jobless, and to issue paper money to pay them. When officials failed to adopt his plan, he organized a march on Washington. One journalist called the march "a petition in boots."

Coxey and about 100 supporters set out from Massilon, Ohio, on March 25, 1894. Sleeping in a circus tent each night, the marchers covered about 15 miles a day. Coxey hoped that thousands of unemployed men would join them along the way. But when the march reached Washington on April 30, "Coxey's Army"consisted of only about 500 people. On May 1, they walked peaceably to the Capitol, where Coxey intended to make a speech on the building's steps. But Washington's police overreacted. They attacked the marchers with clubs, and arrested Coxey. Charged with trampling the grass, he was sentenced to 20 days in jail. Although the "army" lingered in Washington for several weeks, it was ignored by Congress, which provided no relief for the nation's unemployed.

Did you know...

In 1944, 50 years after his march, Coxey was finally allowed to make a speech from the steps of the Capitol.

Before 1750

1750-1799

1800-1849

1850-1899

1900-1924

1925-1949

1950-1974

1975-2000

The Pullman Strike

The Pullman strike

What:
A strike by the American Railway Union (ARU) against the Pullman Palace Car Company ends in violence

When:
May 11–August 3, 1894

Where:
Chicago, Illinois

Illustration: National Guardsmen fire on Pullman Co. strikers in 1894. (The Granger Collection)

"We are working for less wages than will maintain ourselves and our families," said a labor leader at the Pullman Palace Car Co. in Chicago after the company cut its workers' salaries. "There is nothing to arbitrate," said a spokesman for company owner George Pullman, who felt that "a man should have the right to manage his own company." With neither side willing to compromise, a strike was certain. The strike that began in May, 1894, became one of the most violent strikes in history.

Six weeks after 2,500 Pullman workers went on strike, the American Railway Union (ARU) told its members not to work on trains with Pullman cars. Since most trains had a Pullman dining, sleeping, or parlor car, train service throughout the country, including mail delivery, was disrupted. The government ordered an end to the strike, but the strikers were in no mood to listen. When they damaged a train, President Grover Cleveland sent in troops. On July 7, soldiers, National Guardsmen, and police fired on the strikers. Thirteen people were killed and dozens injured. Hundreds were arrested. A federal force began operating the trains, and the strike officially ended on August 3, closing a tragic episode in labor history.

Did you know...

Eugene V. Debs, president of the ARU, was arrested during the strike. He later ran unsuccessfully for U.S. President five times.

The First U.S. Subways

American cities build rail lines underground

When:
Beginning in 1895

Where:
Boston, Massachusetts; and New York City

Illustration: An early New York City subway car reserved for women only. (Culver Pictures)

Before 1750

1750-1799

1800-1849

1850-1899

1900-1924

1925-1949

1950-1974

1975-2000

In the late 1800's, the streets of Boston were clogged with traffic. Horse-drawn streetcars, wagons, carriages, and a few newfangled "horseless carriages" (automobiles) jammed narrow roads first laid out in colonial times. Outside the city, speedy trains carried passengers in comfort. But there was no space for a railway in the heart of the city.

For an answer to its problem, Boston looked across the Atlantic Ocean to London, England. There, starting in the 1860's, a railway had been built underground. So in 1895, Bostonians began to build their own subway system. Workers tore up the streets and dug huge trenches for the tracks. Then the tracks were roofed over and the streets restored. In 1897, the first section of the subway opened to passengers. The underground route became a success, and Boston soon added many more miles to the system.

Meanwhile, New York City struggled with traffic problems too. New Yorkers first tried elevated tracks, which carried trains above city streets. But an elevated system was noisy and darkened the streets below. So New Yorkers decided to build a subway. The first line opened in 1904. Other lines followed, until New York had 700 miles of subway track, more than any other city.

Did you know...

New York City built an experimental subway in 1870. Cars were pushed along 300 feet of track by compressed air.

Comic Strips

Before 1750

1750-1799

1800-1849

1850-1899

1900-1924

1925-1949

1950-1974

1975-2000

Life in America

Comic strips

What:
Series of cartoons that tell a story

When:
First published in newspapers in 1895

Illustration: "Dick Tracy" has been fighting crime since 1931 in one of the most popular comic strips. (Tribune Media Services)

"Peanuts." "Blondie." "Garfield." "Cathy." "Calvin and Hobbes.": Comic strips are among the most popular features in American newspapers. The "funnies" have entertained readers of all ages for more than 100 years.

The first comic strip—a series of cartoons telling a story—appeared in the *New York World* in 1895. Called "Hogan's Alley," it featured the Yellow Kid, a wisecracking little boy. Rival newspapers soon realized that comics could boost sales, and new strips appeared in quick succession. Among the most popular were "The Katzenjammer Kids," featuring two boys who loved to play jokes on adults; "Mutt and Jeff," in which two mismatched fellows traded insults, and "Krazy Kat," whose leading character fell in love with a mean mouse named Ignatz. As the funnies grew in popularity, companies bought the rights to license—or syndicate—strips to newspapers all over the country.

By the 1930's, not all comic strips were "funnies." There were family stories, such as "Gasoline Alley"; science-fiction strips, such as "Flash Gordon"; crime-fighting sagas, such as "Dick Tracy"; and superhero strips, such as "Superman." In 1960, the enormously popular "Peanuts" made its debut. And in 1975, Garry Trudeau's satirical "Doonesbury" became the first comic strip to be awarded a Pulitzer Prize.

Did you know...

Mad Magazine's Alfred E. Newman was based on "The Yellow Kid," an 1895 comic-strip character.

Life in America

The Bicycle Craze

The bicycle craze

What:
A fad for bicycle-riding sweeps the country

When:
1890's

*Illustration: Bicyclers in New York City in the 1890's.
(The Granger Collection)*

Before 1750

1750-1799

1800-1849

1850-1899

1900-1924

1925-1949

1950-1974

1975-2000

Americans went wild for bicycles in the 1890's. Everyone rode—even President William McKinley. His was an ordinary machine, but Lillian Russell, a famous entertainer, rode a gold-plated bike with mother-of-pearl handles.

Across the country, thousands of people joined bicycle clubs. Towns built elevated bicycle paths. There were even bicycle versions of popular dances. Chicago had bicycle ambulances (pairs of bikes, with stretchers in between), and New York's street-cleaning inspectors made their rounds on bikes.

The craze swept the country because bicycles became safe and easy to ride. Early bicycles had a huge front wheel, which was difficult to maneuver. The wheels were made of iron, which made for a very bumpy ride. But in the late 1880's, chain-driven bicycles with two equal-sized wheels were introduced. They were easy to steer, and they had air-filled tires that cushioned the ride. Now almost everyone wanted a bicycle. By 1896, some 250 U.S. factories were turning out more than a million bikes a year. Many of the riders were young women, who enjoyed the freedom that bicycling offered. Most ignored the advice of an etiquette book that cautioned them to put a screen on their bicycles to keep their feet and ankles hidden from view.

Did you know...

The first bicycle was developed in Germany in 1818. It had no foot pedals—the rider pushed himself along with his feet!

Gillette's Razor

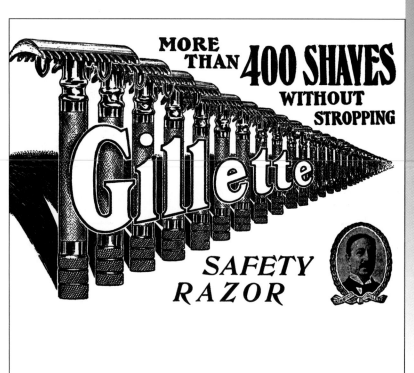

Gillette's razor

What:
A safe, easy-to-use razor with disposable blades

Who:
King C. Gillette, inventor

When:
1895

Where:
Boston, Massachusetts

Illustration: An advertisement for Gillette's safety razor. (The Bettmann Archive)

King C. Gillette was a traveling salesman and an amateur inventor who found shaving a pain in the neck—sometimes literally. In the 1890's, men shaved with straight razors. These long, knifelike blades were cumbersome and dangerous, and they had to be sharpened between shaves. Gillette set out to invent a razor that was safe and easy to use, with blades that would never need sharpening.

The result was the Gillette Safety Razor. This T-shaped shaving tool used a thin, disposable blade attached at a right angle to a short handle. The razor's size and shape made it easy to use, while the handle kept the user's hand away from the cutting edge. When the blade grew dull, it was easily replaced.

Gillette needed six years to bring his invention to market. First, he had to find financial backing and then an engineer who could design equipment to produce the razors. He finally sold his first razor in 1901. Three years later, the invention caught on, and in 1904, the Gillette Safety Razor Company sold 90,000 razors and 12.4 million blades. Gillette had changed America's shaving habits forever and made a fortune doing so.

Did you know...

Since Gillette started production, people have used more than 500 million safety razors and 100 billion blades.

Before 1750

1750-1799

1800-1849

1850-1899

1900-1924

1925-1949

1950-1974

1975-2000

The First Modern Olympics

Before 1750

1750-1799

1800-1849

1850-1899

1900-1924

1925-1949

1950-1974

1975-2000

The first modern Olympics

What:
Athletes from 13 countries, including the U.S., compete for medals

When:
April 6–15, 1896

Where:
Athens, Greece

Illustration: Four Princeton students competed in the 1896 Olympics: F.A. Lane, Herbert Jamison, Robert Garrett, and A. Tyler. (© IOC/Olympic Museum Collection)

In 1996, thousands of athletes from nearly 200 countries competed in the Olympic Games held in Atlanta, Georgia. Satellites beamed the games to millions of TV viewers worldwide. The first modern Olympics—held 100 years earlier—were quite different.

The ancient Greeks had staged amateur athletic competitions at four-year intervals from 776 B.C. to the end of the fourth century A.D.. Late in the nineteenth century, Baron Pierre de Coubertin of France decided to revive the games as a way of promoting sportsmanship and international harmony. Appropriately, the first modern Olympic Games were held in Athens, Greece, in 1896. Just 13 countries participated.

The U.S. was represented by 10 young athletes, who paid their own way. They arrived in Athens a day before the Olympics started and had no time to rest or practice. Nevertheless, James Connolly won the first event: the triple jump. The Americans soon became crowd favorites, winning nine of the ten track and field events they entered. Thus, that small 1896 U.S. team established a tradition of American excellence in the Olympic Games that continues today.

Did you know...

In 1896, winners received a crown of olive leaves—the prize given in ancient Greece—and a silver medal. The first gold medal was awarded in 1908.

21

The Case of Plessy v. Ferguson

Before 1750

1750-1799

1800-1849

1850-1899

1900-1924

1925-1949

1950-1974

1975-2000

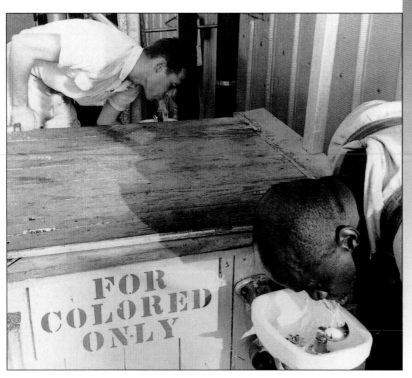

The Case of Plessy v. Ferguson

What:
A U.S. Supreme Court decision that legalized segregation

When:
1896

Where:
Case began in Louisiana; final decision by the U.S. Supreme Court in Washington, D.C.

Illustration: Until the 1950's, blacks and whites drank from separate water fountains in the South. (The Bettmann Archive)

On a June day in 1892, a light-skinned passenger of mixed black and white ancestry was challenged by the conductor of a Louisiana train. "Are you a colored man?" he asked. "Yes," replied Homer Plessy. "Then you will have to retire to the colored car," ordered the conductor. Plessy refused and was arrested. Thus began one of the most famous cases in American law.

Plessy was challenging a Louisiana law of 1890 that required railroads to segregate blacks from whites in "separate but equal" accommodations. When the case was brought before Judge John H. Ferguson of the New Orleans Criminal Court, Ferguson ruled that the Louisiana law was constitutional. Plessy's lawyers then took the suit to the U.S. Supreme Court, arguing that segregation stamped blacks with "a badge of inferiority." But the Supreme Court upheld the Louisiana law by a vote of seven to one.

After the Plessy decision, Southern states passed more segregation laws. African-Americans were kept apart from whites in schools, hospitals, and theaters and on public transportation. They were even required to use separate restrooms and water fountains. Not until 1954, in the case of *Brown v. Board of Education of Topeka*, did the Supreme Court finally rule that "separate but equal" had no place in American society.

Did you know...

Justice John Marshall Harlan, the only Supreme Court justice who voted to oppose the Lousiana segregation law, was a former slave owner from Kentucky.

Notable People

William McKinley, the 25th President

Born:
January 29, 1843, in Niles, Ohio

Term:
March 4, 1897, to September 14, 1901

States:
45

Died:
September 14, 1901

William McKinley

Illustration: This placard from the 1896 election has a movable wheel that could be turned to display McKinley's policies. (The Granger Collection)

Before 1750

1750-1799

1800-1849

1850-1899

1900-1924

1925-1949

1950-1974

1975-2000

William McKinley was a kind, peace-loving man. Yet during his presidency the U.S. went to war against Spain, and three years later his life was ended violently by an assassin's bullet.

A successful lawyer and active Republican, McKinley served as a U.S. congressman and as governor of Ohio. When he became President in 1897, tension with Spain was mounting. The main cause was Cuba, which was rebelling against Spanish rule. Many Americans wanted their army to take the rebels' side, but McKinley tried to find peaceful solutions to the problem. Then, in 1898, the U.S. warship *Maine* mysteriously blew up at Havana, Cuba. The U.S. blamed Spain and declared war. The conflict lasted just 113 days. The victorious U.S. gained control of Puerto Rico and the Philippine Islands. Some Americans objected, saying that a democracy shouldn't build an overseas empire. But most people supported expansion,

and, after many sleepless nights of indecision, so did McKinley. The U.S. also annexed the Hawaiian Islands that same year. McKinley was easily reelected in 1900. But six months after he started his second term, he was shot by Leon Czolgosz, an anarchist who opposed all government. The President died eight days later.

Did you know...

McKinley's 1896 presidential bid was called the "front porch" campaign. He stayed at his home in Ohio, where he addressed voters who traveled there to see him.

Before 1750

1750-1799

1800-1849

1850-1899

1900-1924

1925-1949

1950-1974

1975-2000

The Stanley Steamer

The Stanley Steamer

What:
A steam-powered automobile

When:
Produced from 1897 to 1925

Who:
Designed and manufactured by Francis E.
and Freelan O. Stanley

Where:
Produced in Massachusettes

Illustration: The Stanley Steamer or the "Flying Teapot", a steam-driven automobile produced between 1897 and 1925.

Nearly all of the 200 million automobiles on American roads today are powered by gasoline. But around 1900, when the automobile industry was just beginning, four out of every ten cars were powered by steam. The most famous steam-powered car was the Stanley Steamer, otherwise known as the "Flying Teapot."

The first Stanley Steamer was designed and built in 1897 by Francis and Freelan Stanley, twins who wore identical beards and clothes. Their cars were among the quietest and fastest on the road. A Stanley racing car set a world land-speed record in 1906, racing across the sands at Daytona, Florida, at 127.56 miles an hour. The next year, a Stanley racer was clocked at 150 miles an hour before it crashed.

The peak of Stanley Steamer production came in 1912, when the brothers' Massachusetts factory turned out 650 cars. But gasoline-powered cars with fast electric starters were beginning to take over the market. It took up to 20 minutes to get a Steamer going. Owners had to light the boiler, heat the water, and open a series of valves that one engineer called a "plumber's nightmare." The Stanley twins retired in 1917, and their company went out of business in 1925.

Did you know...

The Stanley Steamer needed no transmission, clutch, gearshift, or spark plugs. Its rear-mounted engine had only 13 moving parts.

Samuel Langley's Aerodrome

Samuel Pierpont Langley, pioneer in aeronautics and astrophysics

Born:
August 22, 1834, in Roxbury, Massachusetts

Died:
February 27, 1906

Illustration: Samuel Langley's the first powered, heavier-than-air flying craft. (UPI/Bettmann)

On May 6, 1896, spectators lined the banks of Washington's Potomac River to watch a grand experiment. Using a catapult on top of a houseboat, Samuel Langley launched his "aerodrome," a 16–foot-long, 25–pound unmanned aircraft with two sets of silk-covered wings. Powered by a steam engine and two propellers, the craft rose 100 feet above the water and flew half a mile down the river before dropping gently to the water. This was the first sustained flight by a heavier-than-air, powered vehicle.

Langley was an astrophysicist whose studies of solar radiation had earlier won him international recognition. In 1887, he had become secretary of the Smithsonian Institution in Washington. There he began studying how surfaces move through the air. Working with model planes powered by rubber bands, he experimented with different designs, until he launched his "aerodome" in 1896.

Langley's efforts to launch an aircraft with a man aboard were not successful, probably because of structural weaknesses in his designs. But he lived to see his dream of manned, powered flight come true when the Wright brothers made their historic flight at Kitty Hawk, North Carolina, in 1903.

Did you know...

The navy's first aircraft carrier, the U.S.S.*Langley*, honored Langley's pioneering work. Langley Air Force Base in Virginia is also named for him.

Before 1750

1750-1799

1800-1849

1850-1899

1900-1924

1925-1949

1950-1974

1975-2000

Klondike Gold Rush National Historical Park

Klondike Gold Rush National Historical Park

Where:
Skagway, Alaska; and Seattle, Washington

When:
Gold rush occurred in 1897–1898; park established in 1976

Illustration: The historic district of Skagway, Alaska, is preserved in Klondike Gold Rush National Historical Park. (National Park Service)

Thousands of would-be prospectors headed north in 1897–1898, seeking gold near the Klondike River in western Canada's Yukon Territory. Only a few of them found riches, but the Klondike gold rush brought settlers to Alaska, which borders the Yukon. The U.S. commemorates that colorful chapter in history in Klondike Gold Rush National Historical Park.

The park is divided into two far-distant parts. One part is Pioneer Square in Seattle, Washington, where many gold-seekers boarded ships heading north. The second is the park's main part, which includes the historic district of Skagway, in southern Alaska, and the 33-mile-long Chilkoot Trail to the Canadian goldfields. The trail into Canada crosses high mountain passes, where many perished.

Before the gold rush petered out in the 1900's, it had turned Skagway into a boomtown. Today, the prospectors are gone, but visitors can wander along the district's wooden sidewalks and enter its restored saloons and shops. The Gold Rush Cemetery is a vivid reminder of the town's rough-and-tumble past. There, some of the most colorful figures of the gold-rush days are buried.

Did you know...

During the gold-rush era, one Canadian official described Skagway as the most outrageously lawless place in the world.

Before 1750

1750-1799

1800-1849

1850-1899

1900-1924

1925-1949

1950-1974

1975-2000

1898

1898

President:
William McKinley

States:
45

Major event:
Spanish-American War

Illustration: Teddy Roosevelt (center) and the Rough Riders fighting in Cuba during the Spanish-American War. (The Granger Collection)

When 1898 began, U.S. newspapers were filled with sensational stories about the Caribbean island of Cuba, then a Spanish colony. The Cubans wanted independence, but according to the newspapers, Spain was repressing the rebellion by torturing Cuban patriots. To show support for the Cubans, President William McKinley sent the battleship *Maine* to Havana harbor. But on February 15, the *Maine* blew up, killing 300 American sailors. The cause of the blast was never determined, but Americans blamed Spain; in April, war was declared.

America won the first battle of the war far from Cuba. On May 1, Admiral George Dewey and his U.S. Navy fleet destroyed a Spanish fleet near Manila Bay in the Philippines, one of Spain's Asian colonies. Other U.S. fleets bombarded Cuba and Spanish-controlled Puerto Rico. The fighting on the ground was brief.

American troops won a series of battles in Cuba in June and July, despite torrid heat and tropical diseases. One volunteer unit, Theodore Roosevelt's Rough Riders, became famous for a hard-fought victory on San Juan Hill in Cuba. By July, the war was over and the U.S. took control of its first overseas territories: Cuba (which became independent four years later), the Philippines (a U.S. possession until 1947), and Puerto Rico. Thus, the U.S. had become a major world power.

Did you know...

The U.S. also annexed the Hawaiian Islands in 1898.

Before 1750

1750-1799

1800-1849

1850-1899

1900-1924

1925-1949

1950-1974

1975-2000

The Spanish-American War

Before 1750

1750-1799

1800-1849

1850-1899

1900-1924

1925-1949

1950-1974

1975-2000

The Spanish-American War

What:
The U.S. defeats Spain in a brief war

When:
April 25-August 12, 1898

Where:
Cuba, Puerto Rico, the Philippines

Illustration: A unit of African-American soldiers fighting near Santiago, Cuba , in June, 1898. (The Granger Collection)

Secretary of State John Hay called the Spanish-American War a "splendid little war." In less than four months in 1898, the U.S. defeated the once-mighty Spain and became a world power.

The war began in the Caribbean, where Cubans were fighting for independence from Spain. Many Americans sympathized with the Cubans, partly because U.S. newspapers exaggerated reports of Spanish cruelty to Cuban patriots. President William McKinley sent the battleship *Maine* to Havana, Cuba, to show his support for the rebels. Then, on February 15, an explosion tore through the ship, killing some 260 American sailors. No one knows why the ship blew up, but the U.S. blamed Spain. War broke out in April.

On May 1, a U.S. naval squadron commanded by Admiral George Dewey destroyed a Spanish fleet at Manila Bay in the Philippines,

Spain's Pacific colony. In July, American ships defeated another Spanish fleet at Santiago, Cuba. Spanish troops fought bravely against the 16,000 American soldiers who invaded Cuba, but were forced to surrender in less than a month. Under the treaty ending the war, Spain gave up Cuba, and the U.S. took over Puerto Rico, the Philippines, and the Pacific island of Guam.

Did you know...

U.S. battle deaths in the Spanish-American War were fewer than 400, but more than 5,000 American troops died from yellow fever and other diseases.

The Sinking of the USS *Maine*

Before 1750

1750-1799

1800-1849

1850-1899

1900-1924

1925-1949

1950-1974

1975-2000

The sinking of the USS Maine

What:
The destruction of an American battleship leads to war with Spain

When:
February 15, 1898

Where:
Havana, Cuba

Illustration: The USS Maine *explodes in the harbor at Havana, Cuba, in 1898. (The Granger Collection)*

On the night of February 15, 1898, the American battleship *Maine* rode quietly at anchor in the harbor of Havana, Cuba. Suddenly, a huge explosion ripped through the ship. The *Maine* split in two and sank to the bottom of the harbor, killing 260 of the men aboard. No one knew for sure what caused the blast, but sensational newspaper reports blamed the Spanish, who controlled Cuba. Within weeks, America and Spain were at war.

Relations between the two countries were tense even before the *Maine* exploded. Cuban rebels had been trying to win independence from Spain for years. Many Americans sympathized with them, especially after U.S. newspapers printed lurid stories about the cruel treatment of the rebels by Spanish authorities. Responding to public pressure, President William McKinley sent the *Maine* to Havana to protest the treatment of the rebels and to pro-

tect American business interests in Cuba.

The sinking of the ship brought public feeling against Spain to the boiling point. McKinley asked Congress to authorize military action, and war was declared on April 25. The slogan "Remember the *Maine*!" rallied the country to the fight.

Did you know...

Many historians doubt that a Spanish mine blew up the *Maine*. The blast may have started in the ship's ammunition stores.

29

Battle of Manila Bay

Battle of Manila Bay

What:
U.S. warships commanded by Commodore
George Dewey win the first battle of the
Spanish-American War

When:
May 1, 1898

Where:
Manila Bay, Philippine Islands

Illustration: The Battle of Manila Bay, which took
place May 1, 1898. (The Granger Collection)

For months, trouble had been brewing between the U.S. and Spain. American newspapers claimed that the Spanish were treating rebels cruelly in Cuba, the Spanish colony that lay just 90 miles south of Florida. Then on February 15, 1898, the U.S. battleship *Maine* blew up in the harbor of Havana, Cuba. No one knows for sure what caused the explosion, but the U.S. blamed Spain and declared war on April 25. Halfway around the world, American naval officer George Dewey sprang into action. Commodore Dewey sailed his six-ship American squadron across the South China Sea toward the Philippine Islands, another Spanish possession. His fleet entered Manila Bay on the evening of April 30.

Aboard his flagship *Olympia*, Dewey gave the order to attack the Spanish fleet at dawn on May 1: "You may fire when you are ready, Gridley." Although threatened by shore batteries, the American ships had more firepower than the aging Spanish vessels. By noon, the Spanish ships were destroyed and 381 Spaniards were dead or wounded. Not a single American was killed in action.

Did you know...

After the Battle of Manila Bay, the U.S. took control of the Philippines. The islands, which were captured by the Japanese during World War II, became an independent nation in 1946.

Before 1750

1750-1799

1800-1849

1850-1899

1900-1924

1925-1949

1950-1974

1975-2000

The U.S. Takes Over the Philippines

The U.S. takes over the Philippines

What:
The U.S. takes control of the Philippines during the Spanish-American War

When:
1898

Where:
The Philippine Islands, in the Western Pacific

Illustration: American troops in Manila, the capital of the Philippines, in 1898. (Brown Brothers)

In 1898, the U.S. went to war with Spain. Independence for Cuba, which Spain then controlled, was the main issue of the war. But the conflict quickly spread to other Spanish colonies, including the Philippine Islands in the Western Pacific. There, U.S. Navy ships under Commodore George Dewey defeated a Spanish fleet at the Battle of Manila Bay on May 1. In the weeks that followed, U.S. troops, along with Filipino rebels opposed to Spanish rule, took control of the islands.

The triumphant Filipinos, believing that the U.S. supported their struggle, declared independence. But under the treaty that ended the Spanish-American War on December 10, 1898, Spain turned the Philippines over to the U.S. for a payment of $20 million. America thus became an imperial power—a country that controls another. Some Americans were delighted, but others did not believe that a democratic nation should hold control other lands.

Filipino revolutionaries, led by Emilio Aguinaldo, fought U.S. forces for two years. After an uneasy peace was established, the islands began a transition to self-government that ended with full independence in 1946.

Did you know...

Filipinos celebrate their independence on July 12, the date in 1898 when Emilio Aguinaldo first declared the islands independent from Spain.

Before 1750

1750-1799

1800-1849

1850-1899

1900-1924

1925-1949

1950-1974

1975-2000

The Takeover of Puerto Rico

Before 1750

1750-1799

1800-1849

1850-1899

1900-1924

1925-1949

1950-1974

1975-2000

Important Events

The takeover of Puerto Rico

What:
U.S. troops invade Puerto Rico during the Spanish-American War

Where:
Guanica Bay, Puerto Rico

When:
July 25, 1898

Illustration: U.S. troops in Ponce, Puerto Rico, during the Spanish-American War. (The Granger Collection)

The U.S. went to war against Spain in 1898 primarily to free Cuba from its long and harsh domination by the Spanish. But many Americans viewed the war as a good excuse to gain new possessions for the U.S. And Puerto Rico, an island 1,000 miles southeast of Florida, was the closest Spanish colony that American expansionists desired.

In May, 1898, while a U.S. Navy fleet was destroying a Spanish fleet in the Philippines, and another was fighting near Cuba, seven American warships appeared off the coast of Puerto Rico and fired on El Morro, the old fort guarding the capital city of San Juan. Then the ships sailed away. Two months later, however, the U.S. landed thousands of troops at Guanica Bay on Puerto Rico's southern coast. They quickly defeated the weak Spanish garrison on the island. Many Puerto Ricans welcomed the Americans, hoping they would help the island become independent.

The Spanish-American War lasted only five months. In the peace treaty, Spain agreed to accept $20 million from the U.S. for Puerto Rico and the Pacific island of Guam. Soon afterward, the Americans established a military government on Puerto Rico, and the island's residents became U.S. citizens in 1917. Then in 1953, Puerto Rico became a self-governing commonwealth, "freely associated" with the U.S.

Did you know...

In 1993, Puerto Ricans voted to remain a commonwealth rather than become the 51st state or an independent nation.

America at War

The Rough Riders

What:
A colorful cavalry unit becomes famous during the Spanish-American War

When:
Summer of 1898

Where:
Cuba

Who:
Led by Teddy Roosevelt, future U.S. President

The Rough Riders

Illustration: Teddy Roosevelt and the Rough Riders in Cuba in 1898. (The Bettmann Archive)

Before 1750

1750-1799

1800-1849

1850-1899

1900-1924

1925-1949

1950-1974

1975-2000

On July 1, 1898, during the brief Spanish-American War, a group of U.S. soldiers known as the Rough Riders stormed up Kettle Hill, a key Spanish position near the city of Santiago, Cuba. Despite heavy gunfire from defending Spanish forces, the Americans captured the hill. Newspaper reports of their victory made the Rough Riders national heroes and launched their leader, Teddy Roosevelt, on the road to the presidency.

The official name of the Rough Riders was the First U.S. Volunteer Cavalry Regiment. The unit was founded by Colonel Leonard Wood when war broke out in April, 1898; its members included cowboys and lawmen from the West and wealthy socialites and sportsmen from the East. One journalist referred to the rowdy unit as "the society page, financial column, and Wild West Show all wrapped up in one." Roosevelt resigned as assistant secretary of the

navy to join the group in May, and became its commander in June.

When the regiment sailed for Cuba, there was no room for their horses on the ship. So the charge up Kettle Hill was made on foot, not horseback. Because the Rough Riders and their leader were so colorful, they received extensive press coverage. They returned home in August, and that fall, Roosevelt was elected governor of New York.

Did you know...

Teddy Roosevelt was elected Vice President in 1900 and became President when William McKinley was assassinated in 1901.

33

Walter Reed

Walter Reed, physician and pioneer in the control of infectious diseases

Born:
September 13, 1851, in Belroi, Virginia

Died:
November 22, 1902

Illustration: Walter Reed (center) in Cuba in 1900. (The Granger Collection)

Before 1750

1750-1799

1800-1849

1850-1899

1900-1924

1925-1949

1950-1974

1975-2000

Walter Reed was just 17 years old when he received his medical degree from the University of Virginia. He then joined the U.S. Army Medical Corps and became a high-ranking surgeon. But in the early 1900's, he turned his attention to a new field of research: bacteriology, the study of germs. Reed became an expert on the identification and isolation of germs and played a key role in wiping out two deadly diseases, typhoid fever and yellow fever.

In 1898, during the Spanish-American War, Reed was commissioned to study the origin and spread of typhoid in army camps. His experiments showed that flies carried the infection and that unsanitary conditions allowed the disease to spread. Two years later, Reed was sent to Cuba to combat a yellow-fever epidemic among U.S. soldiers. A Cuban doctor named Carlos Finlay had already theorized that the disease was spread by mosquitoes. But most people did not believe him. Instead, they shunned yellow-fever victims and burned their homes and belongings. Reed conducted a series of experiments with "human guinea pigs," who volunteered to be infected. He proved that only mosquito bites could cause the disease. When the mosquitoes' breeding grounds were drained, the epidemic ended. Because of Reed's findings, the U.S. was able to build the Panama Canal with greatly reduced fear of yellow fever.

Did you know...

The U.S. Army's Medical Center in Washington, D.C., is named for Reed.

The U.S. Annexes Hawaii

Before 1750

1750-1799

1800-1849

1850-1899

1900-1924

1925-1949

1950-1974

1975-2000

The U.S. annexes Hawaii

What:
The U.S. formally takes over the Hawaiian Islands

When:
August 12, 1898

Illustration: An 1897 newspaper cartoon shows Hawaii as a reluctant bride, marrying Uncle Sam. President McKinley is the best man, and planter Sanford Dole gives the bride away. (The Granger Collection)

On August 12, 1898, gunfire echoed throughout Honolulu, the capital of Hawaii. It was not the sound of battle, but a 21-gun salute announcing the annexation of Hawaii by the United States. Americans in the islands cheered the event, but it marked the end of independence for native Hawaiians.

Americans first settled in Hawaii after British explorer James Cook's visit there in 1778. The Americans became wealthy raising sugar and pineapples for export. As their wealth and power grew, they took political and economic control of the islands from the native people. When Queen Liliuokalani ascended to the Hawaiian throne in 1891, she tried to reduce the American planters' power. But U.S. Marines helped them overthrow the queen in 1893. The planters declared Hawaii a republic, and named Sanford B. Dole, an American pineapple grower, president. The new govern-

ment quickly negotiated a treaty of annexation with the U.S.

When Grover Cleveland became President in March, 1893, he determined that most Hawaiians did not want annexation and withdrew the treaty. But William McKinley, the next president, agreed to annexation, which occurred in 1898. Hawaii became a U.S. territory in 1900, and the 50th state in 1959.

Did you know...

Hawaii is the only state that was once a monarchy. Kamehameha I united the islands in 1795 and became the first king.

Guam

Guam, a U.S. territory

Where:
An island in the Mariana chain in the west central Pacific Ocean

When:
Captured by the U.S. in 1898

Area:
209 square miles

Capital:
Agana

Population:
133,152

Illustration: Guam, a U.S. territory in the Pacific. (Superstock)

Three thousand miles west of Hawaii lies a small U.S. territory known for its idyllic beaches and pleasant climate. Temperatures average an ideal 80 degrees year-round on Guam. Rustling sword grass carpets the island's volcanic hills. And a thick rain forest covers the island's northern lowlands.

Sailing under the Spanish flag, Ferdinand Magellan discovered this 209-square-mile island in 1521. The U.S. captured it in 1898, during the Spanish-American War, and it has remained an important U.S. military base. In 1950, Guam became an unincorporated U.S. territory. Its 150,000 people are called Guamanians. They are U.S. citizens but are not permitted to vote in presidential elections.

The first inhabitants of Guam were the Chamorros, who originated in Malaysia and Indonesia in about 1500 B.C. Some of their descendants still speak the Chamorro dialect in

their homes, but everyone speaks English at work and school. Before Guam became a U.S. military base, Guamanians lived in small farming and fishing villages. Today, most work at one of the island's many military facilities. As a result, Guam now imports most of its food. Tourism is the second most important industry. Each year, thousands of tourists visit Guam to enjoy the island's luxury resorts.

Did you know...

Japan seized Guam early in World War II. The United States recaptured the island in 1944.

Before 1750 | 1750-1799 | 1800-1849 | 1850-1899 | 1900-1924 | 1925-1949 | 1950-1974 | 1975-2000

Famous Places

Puerto Rico

The Commonwealth of Puerto Rico

Capital:
San Juan

Ceded to U.S. :
1898

Commonwealth status:
1952

Population:
3,522,037

Area:
3,435 square miles

Illustration: Condado Beach in San Juan, Puerto Rico.
(© Robert Frerck/Woodfin Camp)

Before 1750

1750-1799

1800-1849

1850-1899

1900-1924

1925-1949

1950-1974

1975-2000

When Columbus made his second voyage to the New World in 1493, he landed on a beautiful, mountainous island in the Caribbean. He called the island "San Juan," and its natural harbor "Puerto Rico," Spanish for "Rich Port." Later, Puerto Rico became the designation of the entire island, and the name San Juan was given to its capital.

Fifteen years after Columbus' visit, Ponce de León established a Spanish colony there. Most of the Arawak Indians, the original inhabitants, died from diseases introduced by the Europeans. Gradually, Puerto Rico became an important Spanish possession, linking Spain with its colonies in Latin America. In 1898, when the U.S. won the Spanish-American War, Spain ceded Puerto Rico to the U.S. All Puerto Ricans became American citizens in 1917, and the island became a commonwealth in 1952. Puerto Ricans elect their own governor and legislature, but cannot vote in U.S. presidential elections.

The cultural and political center of the island is the capital, San Juan. In the old part of the city, crooked cobblestone streets and old colonial buildings are reminders of the island's rich Spanish heritage. Puerto Rico's white sand beaches, tropical climate, and lush rain forest have made tourism the biggest industry. The island exports sugarcane, citrus fruits, coffee, and other products.

Did you know...

Puerto Rico is the only piece of U.S. territory on which Columbus actually set foot.

Holland's Submarine

Before 1750

1750-1799

1800-1849

1850-1899

1900-1924

1925-1949

1950-1974

1975-2000

Holland's submarine

What:
The first practical submarine

Who:
John Philip Holland, inventor

When:
Launched in 1898

Where:
J.P. Holland Torpedo Boat Company, Paterson, New Jersey

Illustration: The submarine Holland, *built for the U.S. Navy in 1898. (Brown Brothers)*

Even before 1800, navy men had dreamed of a ship that could travel underwater. They had devised crude one-person submarines, but the little subs usually sank before they could attack enemy vessels. Then, in the mid-1800's, inventors began to develop technologies that would lead to the modern submarine. The most successful of these inventors was John Holland.

As a young man in Ireland, Holland began experimenting with underwater ships, hoping that the Irish could someday use submarines against the British, who ruled Ireland. In 1872, Holland immigrated to New Jersey, where he continued to develop his idea, supported by Irish revolutionaries. After 20 years, he built the 31-foot-long *Fenian Ram*, the first successful submarine. It was never used in Ireland, but the U.S. Navy asked Holland to build several larger craft. In 1898, he launched the *Holland*, a 53-foot cigar-shaped sub with a steel hull and a single torpedo tube. It carried a crew of nine, and could travel on the surface using a gasoline engine or underwater using electrical batteries. The success of the *Holland* brought orders from England, Russia, and Japan, as well as the U.S. Holland died in 1914. That same year, submarines began playing a serious military role in World War I, changing naval warfare forever.

Did you know...

Holland also invented a respirator to help sailors escape from disabled submarines.

American Samoa

American Samoa, U.S. territory

Where:
In the south-central Pacific Ocean, about 2,300 miles Southwest of Hawaii

When:
Acquired in 1899

Population:
46,773

Area:
76 square miles

Capital:
Pago Pago

Illustration: The harbor at Pago Pago in American Samoa. (© George Holton/Photo Researchers, Inc.)

"Sheer beauty, so pure, it is difficult to breathe it in." That's how the English poet Rupert Brooke once described the Pacific islands that today form American Samoa. The Samoan people understand his reaction. They are proud of their beautiful tropical home and their easygoing lifestyle, which they call *Fa'asamoa*—"the Samoan way."

American Samoa includes seven small islands, the tips of ancient volcanoes that rose from the ocean floor. Tutuila is the largest island and the site of the capital, Pago Pago. Centuries ago, Polynesians settled on these islands. The culture they developed revolved around villages, each controlled by a chief. In the late 1800's, the Samoan chiefs gave the U.S. permission to set up a naval refueling station at Pago Pago. The islands became a U.S. territory through an international treaty in 1899.

The territory's governor and its legislature, the Fono, are elected by the Samoans. Village chiefs still play an important role in society, and other traditions remain strong. Many Samoans today work in the islands' tuna-packing industry. Others work in the thriving tourist trade, greeting visitors with a warm *talofa* ("hello") and making them feel at home in this island paradise.

Did you know...

Traditional Samoan village homes are thatch houses called *fales*. A wraparound cloth called a *lavalava* is the traditional dress.

Before 1750

1750-1799

1800-1849

1850-1899

1900-1924

1925-1949

1950-1974

1975-2000

Steelmaking in America

Steelmaking in America

What:
America develops its steel industry

When:
Late 1800's

Where:
Pennsylvania, Ohio, Indiana

Illustration: A painting of an early steel mill by Aaron H. Gorson. (Collection of Mellon Bank)

In the 1850's, railroads began to crisscross the U.S. The builders of these railroads used rails and locomotives made of iron. But although iron was strong, it was brittle. Steel—iron that has been purified and mixed with a tiny amount of carbon—was much better, but was too expensive. Then, in 1856, Henry Bessemer in England and William Kelly in the U.S. hit on a new, cheaper process for making steel.

The first U.S. steel mills using the new process opened near Bethlehem and Pittsburgh, Pennsylvania. They used huge amounts of coal from nearby mines to heat iron ore to a molten, or liquid, state. Air was then blown through the red-hot liquid, burning off impurities. Finally, the right amount of carbon was added and the metal was poured into molds to cool.

Andrew Carnegie, a young businessman, saw the promise of the steel industry. Between 1870 and 1900, he assembled a huge network of iron mines, coal mines, and steel mills, becoming one of the richest and most powerful men in the country as a result. Builders began to use steel for long bridges and ever-taller buildings, and, in the early 1900's, the demand for automobiles greatly expanded the market. Through the 1960's, steelmaking was one of the most important U.S. industries.

Did you know...

Many steel mills were built near the Great Lakes so they could receive iron ore by barge from Minnesota.

Before 1750

1750-1799

1800-1849

1850-1899

1900-1924

1925-1949

1950-1974

1975-2000

The Boxer Rebellion

The Boxer Rebellion

What:
American troops help put down a violent Chinese uprising

When:
1900

Where:
China

Illustration: American troops in Beijing during the Boxer Rebellion of 1900. (Culver Pictures)

In 1900, U.S. soldiers joined an eight-nation force that rushed to the aid of foreigners in China. Americans and other westerners there were being attacked by violent gangs in an uprising known as the Boxer Rebellion.

The uprising grew out of a wave of anti-foreign feeling that swept China in the late 1800's. Britain, the United States, and other countries had signed trade pacts with China that many Chinese felt were unfair. As Western domination grew, some Chinese feared their country would be permanently divided and ruled by foreigners. Members of a secret society called Boxers were among the strongest opponents of Western influence.

The Boxer Rebellion broke out in 1899, in northern China. With the secret support of the empress of China, gangs attacked Westerners and killed Chinese Christians. In Beijing, the capital, foreign diplomats and merchants, and

their families were besieged by gangs. In June, the international rescue force arrived in China and by mid-August, had crushed the rebellion. China later agreed to pay more than $300 million in damages and punish the rebellion's leaders.

Did you know...

The Boxers called themselves the Righteous and Harmonious Fists. Americans called them Boxers because they did exercises that looked like boxing.

Before 1750

1750-1799

1800-1849

1850-1899

1900-1924

1925-1949

1950-1974

1975-2000

Breakfast Cereals

Illustration: Cereal flakes (left) replaced oatmeal as America's favorite breakfast food. (Culver Pictures, Inc.; The Granger Collection)

Wheat, rice, oats, or corn . . . flaked, ground, rolled, puffed, or shredded . . . with sugar, honey, raisins, nuts, dates, or marshmallow bits—Americans can choose from dozens of different breakfast cereals. There are enough varieties to fill an entire aisle in most supermarkets.

Until the late 1800's, breakfast cereals were whole-grain products, such as oatmeal, meant to be cooked and served hot. The first dry, flaked cereals were developed in Battle Creek, Michigan, by Dr. John H. Kellogg, who encouraged a meatless diet that was rich in grains. Supposedly, the first cornflakes were made when a pot of grain boiled over on the stove, and some of the grain dried into crispy bits.

Kellogg thought of flaked cereal as a health food. But Charles Post and Will Kellogg, James' brother, had bigger ideas. Around 1900, each founded a company to produce cereal flakes as a breakfast food for everyone. Since then, hundreds of cereals have been introduced. In our fast-paced society, many families appreciate being able to pour their breakfasts from a box—especially parents of young children. Cereal companies try to appeal to youngsters by offering a variety of sweetened cereals in amusing shapes, packed in boxes featuring cartoon characters, sports stars, and prizes.

Did you know...

To make puffed rice and wheat, the grain is shot out of a cannon-like device; steam pressure is built up inside it and the kernels puff up when the pressure is released.

Before 1750

1750-1799

1800-1849

1850-1899

1900-1924

1925-1949

1950-1974

1975-2000

A Year to Remember

1901

Presidents:
William McKinley, Theodore Roosevelt

States:
45

Major event:
Assassination of President McKinley

Illustration: Leon Czolgosz shoots President McKinley on September 6, 1901. (The Granger Collection)

1901

On September 6, 1901, President William McKinley greeted the public at a reception in Buffalo, New York. He was there to speak at the Pan American Exposition about America's growing role as a world power. But as he reached out to shake the hand of an apparent well-wisher, two shots rang out and the President staggered backward.

The shots were fired by Leon Czolgosz, an anarchist (one who opposes all government). He had vowed to kill a "great ruler," and he succeeded. The President clung to life for eight days, but died on September 14. That day, Vice President Theodore Roosevelt was sworn in as President. Czolgosz was promptly tried, convicted, and executed.

The September assassination of the President cast a pall over a year that had begun well. The country was prosperous and at peace. And it had gained overseas posses-sions—Puerto Rico and the Philippines—in the Spanish-American War of 1898. As a result, the U.S. had new importance in the world. After McKinley's death, Roosevelt rallied the shaken country. At 42, he was the youngest person to serve as President. His energy and talent for leadership soon made him one of the most popular and influential leaders in U.S. history.

Did you know...

In the year 1901, drillers also made the first major oil strike in Texas, near Beaumont.

Spindletop

Important Events

The Spindletop oil strike

What:
A "gusher" sets off America's first major oil rush

When:
January 10, 1901

Where:
Near Beaumont, Texas

Illustration: Oil gushes from a well at Spindletop, near Beaumont, Texas, in 1906. (The Granger Collection)

For nine years, prospectors had probed the earth at Spindletop Mound, near Beaumont, Texas, in search of oil. Many experts scoffed at the idea that there was oil to be found in Texas. But on January 10, 1901, the patience of the prospectors paid off. As a drill probed more than 1,000 feet below the surface, the ground began to shake. Then, with a roar, a fountain of "black gold" shot out of the earth and rained down on the startled drillers. No one had ever seen oil gush from the ground like that.

Demand for oil to light kerosene lamps and power internal-combustion engines had been growing rapidly at the start of the 1900's. People realized there were fortunes to be made by those who could supply it. So word of the Spindletop strike spread quickly, and America's first major oil rush was on. Within a year, more than 100 small companies and "wildcatters"—independent drillers—were on the scene. An

acre of land once worth $10 now sold for $900,000! The boom ended within a few years, when the Spindletop oil field dried up. But wildcatters set out across the state in search of new fields. And by 1928, Texas led the nation in oil production.

Did you know...

An oil-company executive, who had refused to invest in Spindletop because he did not believe there was oil in Texas, had offered "to drink every gallon of oil found west of the Mississippi."

Theodore Roosevelt

Theodore Roosevelt, 26th President of the United States

Born:
October 27, 1868, in New York City

Term:
1901–1909

Home:
Sagamore Hill, Oyster Bay, New York

Died:
January 6, 1919

Illustration: President Theodore Roosevelt. (© The White House Historical Association: Photographed by the National Geographic Society)

"Do you know the two most wonderful things I have seen in your country?" a foreign visitor once asked an American. "Niagara Falls and the President of the United States...both great wonders of nature."

That President was Theodore Roosevelt, usually referred to as "Teddy." He was a bundle of energy, who loved participating in the "strenuous life" of a cowboy and big-game hunter. He had been Police Commissioner of New York City, Governor of New York, Assistant Secretary of the Navy, and a leader of troops in the Spanish-American War. He was elected Vice President in 1900, and became President in 1901 when William McKinley was assassinated.

As President, Roosevelt launched a "trust busting" campaign against big business. An ardent conservationist, he set aside thousands of square miles of woodlands as national parks and forests. In foreign affairs, Roosevelt's greatest achievement was the Panama Canal, which was begun under his leadership. For helping to end a war between Russia and Japan, he was awarded the Nobel Prize for Peace. In 1912, Roosevelt formed his own "Bull Moose" Party to try to win a third term as President, but he lost to Woodrow Wilson.

Did you know...

The teddy bear is named for Theodore Roosevelt.

Before 1750

1750-1799

1800-1849

1850-1899

1900-1924

1925-1949

1950-1974

1975-2000

Sagamore Hill

Before 1750

1750-1799

1800-1849

1850-1899

1900-1924

1925-1949

1950-1974

1975-2000

Sagamore Hill

What:
President Theodore Roosevelt's Long Island
home

When:
Built in 1885

Where:
Oyster Bay, Long Island, New York

*Illustration: The North Room of Teddy Roosevelt's
home in Oyster Bay, New York. (© Superstock)*

"Fond as I am of the White House," President Theodore Roosevelt once said, "there isn't any place in the world like home—like Sagamore Hill." Roosevelt's love of his Long Island home was boundless, and the house remains a telling reflection of its larger-than-life owner.

Built for comfort rather than style, the three-story gabled house stands on more than 60 acres, with sweeping porches overlooking Oyster Bay and Long Island Sound. Roosevelt built the house for his first wife, Alice, but she died in 1884 while the house was in construction. After Roosevelt married Edith Carow in 1886, Sagamore Hill became home for them and their family, which eventually included six children. Sagamore Hill was the summer White House during Roosevelt's presidency (1901–1909), and he died there in 1919. It has been maintained by the National Park Service since 1964.

Except for Edith Roosevelt's drawing room, Sagamore Hill's 22 rooms are all Teddy. They are filled with heavy furniture, wood paneling, hunting trophies, and the souvenirs of Roosevelt's adventures. In the huge North Room are Roosevelt's special treasures—his Rough Riders sword and hat from the Spanish-American War, his books, and a set of elephant tusks.

Did you know...

Sagamore Hill was named for Sagamore Mohannis, a Native American who once lived on the land where the house stands.

The Air Conditioner

The air conditioner

What:
A machine that cools indoor air

Who:
Invented by Willis Carrier, engineer and industrialist

When:
1902

Where:
Buffalo, New York

Illustration: A 1958 advertisement for a home air conditioner; bidirectional cooling points cold air toward adjacent rooms. (Corbis-Bettmann)

Outside, the temperature is 98 degrees, and the humidity is unbearable. Inside, everyone is cool and comfortable—thanks to air-conditioning. Air conditioners cool nearly all American offices and stores, and many homes and cars. With air-conditioning, people can almost ignore summer's sweltering heat.

Willis Carrier, an American inventor, developed the first air conditioner in 1902 after observing fog on a cool night. Carrier saw that as air temperatures dropped, water vapor condensed into tiny droplets, forming fog. He realized that by blowing air past cold water or another chilled substance, he could both cool the air and cause moisture to condense and drop away, thereby lowering the humidity. Carrier's first air conditioners were not meant for human comfort. They were designed for bakeries, print shops, and factories where the quality of products depended on steady tempera-

tures and humidity levels. The era of "comfort cooling" began in 1917, when the Empire Theater in Montgomery, Alabama, installed air-conditioning. Hundreds of theaters and stores across the country soon followed the theater's lead. Carrier's "Igloo" model, introduced at the 1939 World's Fair in New York, was the first air conditioner designed for home use.

Did you know...

Scientists have warned that fluorocarbons, the cooling agents used in air conditioners, are harmful to the ozone layer. Researchers are experimenting with alternate refrigerants.

Before 1750

1750-1799

1800-1849

1850-1899

1900-1924

1925-1949

1950-1974

1975-2000

Early Days of Ice Hockey

Before 1750

1750-1799

1800-1849

1850-1899

1900-1924

1925-1949

1950-1974

1975-2000

Early days of ice hockey

When:
Invented in the mid-1850's; rules established in the 1870's

Where:
Invented in Canada; early U.S. teams in Michigan, New York, Washington, Massachusetts, and Pennsylvania

Illustration: The 1917 Seattle Metropolitans, first U.S. winners of the Stanley Cup. (Hockey Hall of Fame)

The world's fastest team sport, ice hockey was invented in the mid-nineteenth century by British soldiers serving in Canada. In the game's early days, as many as 16 men played on a side. There were no nets, the goalies wore no padding, and the puck was square. But by the 1880's, the sport had begun to resemble the modern game. Amateur hockey leagues formed. And beginning in 1893, a silver trophy called the Stanley Cup was awarded each year to Canada's best hockey team.

Inevitably, ice hockey teams formed in the U.S., especially in the states bordering Canada. Canadians attending Yale and Johns Hopkins universities introduced the game to their classmates. And in 1903, J.L. Gibson, a Michigan dentist, recruited some top Canadian players to form the first professional hockey club. In 1917, the Seattle Metropolitans stunned Canadians, becoming the first U.S. team to win the Stanley Cup. That same year, the National Hockey League (NHL) was born. The Boston Bruins became the league's first U.S. franchise in 1924. Although in later years most NHL teams were based in U.S. cities, Canadian players continued to dominate the sport. Hockey became increasingly popular in the U.S., as new fans discovered the fast-paced, rough, and exciting game.

Did you know...

The Stanley Cup was first donated by Lord Stanley, Canada's governor-general. He paid $48.33 for the original trophy.

The Wright Brothers Learn to Fly

Orville and Wilbur Wright, inventors

What:
The first powered flights

Where:
Kitty Hawk, North Carolina

When:
December 17, 1903

Illustration: History's first powered flight, photographed in 1903. Orville Wright is the pilot. Wilbur Wright watches. (The Granger Collection)

On the morning of December 17, 1903, on the windy dunes at Kitty Hawk in North Carolina, Orville Wright made the first manned and powered flight.

Orville and his brother Wilbur operated a bicycle shop in Dayton, Ohio. They had been dreaming about flying since the 1890's. They were not trained scientists or engineers, but they made a scientific study of the problems of flight. They built and tested gliders to understand the principles of flying. They created a wind tunnel in the bicycle shop to test wing designs, and they studied propeller designs and control mechanisms. Their machinist built a 12-horsepower gasoline engine for them. By 1903, the brothers had built a twin-winged airplane, the *Flyer,* and they felt confident it would fly.

At Kitty Hawk, they constructed a wooden track down a hill to provide a smooth surface for takeoff. With Orville at the controls, Wilbur guided the plane down the track, and it bounded into the air. After covering 40 yards in 12 seconds, it landed gently in the sand. Before the day was out, the brothers had made three more flights, one of which lasted almost a minute. Man, at last, had learned to fly.

Did you know...

The Wright *Flyer* had twin pusher propellers driven by two bicycle chains from the brothers' shop.

The Early Movies

Arts & Entertainment

The movies become America's favorite entertainment

When:
First short films in 1890's; became widely popular in 1900's

Where:
U.S. moviemakers moved to Hollywood, California, beginning in 1908

Illustration: Mack Sennett's hilarious "Keystone Cops" (Movie Still Archives)

In the early 1900's, all you needed was a projector, a sheet to use as a screen, some chairs, and an empty storefront. Then you could open a "nickelodeon" and collect five cents apiece from all the people who wanted to see the newest form of popular entertainment, the movies.

The first movies, just a few minutes long, showed everyday scenes: a sneeze, a kiss, a train. But then the "flickers" began to tell stories. In 1903, crowds flocked to the *Great Train Robbery*, which tells, in 12 minutes, the story of a gang of outlaws who rob a train and are then chased and gunned down by a posse. By 1908, there were more than 10,000 nickelodeons in the U.S. alone, serving more than 25 million customers each week. Movies grew longer and more ambitious. And ornate theaters called "picture palaces" were built to show the expensive dramatic epics created by D.W. Griffith and others.

People went to the movies for thrills and laughter. Audiences especially loved the slapstick comedies produced by Mack Sennett at the Keystone Studios in Hollywood beginning in 1912. Those films featured the wacky "Keystone Kops", and always included a wild chase during which everything that could go wrong did. Audiences didn't care that the films were silent; they often laughed too loud to hear dialogue.

Did you know...

Charlie Chaplin, the great comedian, began his career in Sennett's Keystone comedies.

50

1904

Before 1750

1750-1799

1800-1849

1850-1899

1900-1924

1925-1949

1950-1974

1975-2000

1904

President:
Theodore Roosevelt

States:
45

Major events:
Louisiana Purchase Exposition; Theodore Roosevelt is elected to a full term as President

THE BIG STICK IN THE CARIBBEAN SEA

Illustration: A 1904 cartoon shows President Theodore Roosevelt wielding the "big stick" of American power in the Caribbean region. (The Granger Collection)

"Meet me in St. Louis, Louis, meet me at the fair." That song was heard all over the U.S. in 1904—the year of the Louisiana Purchase Exposition in St. Louis, Missouri. All summer, Americans flocked to the fair, which marked the 100th anniversary of the U.S. purchase of 828,000 square miles of land from France in 1803, doubling the size of the U.S. Products from around the world were on display. Two of the most popular items were new foods that helped visitors beat the heat: iced tea and ice-cream cones.

President Theodore Roosevelt officially opened the fair in May. As President William McKinley's Vice President, Roosevelt had become President suddenly in 1901 when McKinley was assassinated. When Roosevelt ran for President in 1904, he was extremely popular. The voters liked his "big stick" policy—his threat to use force against any foreign power that tried to interfere with U.S. control of the Western Hemisphere. And they liked his new agreement with Panama, which gave the U.S. the right to build a canal in that Central American country, thereby linking the Atlantic Ocean to the Pacific. Roosevelt easily defeated the Democratic candidate, Alton B. Parker, in the November election.

Did you know...

Cy Young pitched baseball's first "perfect game" in 1904; not a single batter reached first base. And at the Olympic Games, held in St. Louis, U.S. athletes took gold medals in all but one of the 22 events.

The *General Slocum* Disaster

The General Slocum Disaster

What:
Fire erupts on an excursion boat, killing more than 1,000 people

Where:
The East River, New York City

When:
June 15, 1904

Illustration: The General Slocum, *an excursion boat, burns in New York Harbor in 1904. (UPI/Corbis-Bettmann)*

On a sunny June morning in 1904, the *General Slocum*, an excursion boat, sailed from Manhattan's Third Street pier, bound for Long Island. Aboard the steamer was a local church group looking forward to a day of picnicking and fun. But just minutes after the *Slocum* left its dock, black smoke began pouring from the ship. Hay and cans of oil had somehow ignited in a supply room, and fire roared through the steamer. The burning of the *Slocum* proved to be one of the worst disasters on water in American history: 1,021 people—mostly women and children—were killed.

One error after another contributed to the day's tragedy. The ship's captain had not trained his crew to handle a fire. Lifeboats, tied to the ship with wire, couldn't be launched. Aging fire hoses burst when the water was turned on, and rotted life preservers sank like weights. Many people jumped overboard to escape the spreading flames and drowned.

The disaster shocked the nation, and President Theodore Roosevelt ordered an investigation. As a result, a federal commission recommended that all new ships be built of steel and have fireproof walls.

Did you know...

A cemetery in Middle Village, New York, contains a monument honoring the dead from the *Slocum* fire. Each year, on June 15, a memorial service is held in their honor.

Before 1750

1750-1799

1800-1849

1850-1899

1900-1924

1925-1949

1950-1974

1975-2000

Teddy Roosevelt Wins the 1906 Nobel Peace Prize

Teddy Roosevelt wins the Nobel Peace Prize

What:
President Theodore Roosevelt helps end the Russo-Japanese War and wins the Nobel Peace Prize

When:
Peace treaty signed on September 6, 1905

Where:
Treaty negotiated in Portsmouth, New Hampshire

Illustration: A political cartoon showing Teddy Roosevelt (center) bringing together the czar of Russia and the emperor of Japan in 1905. (The Granger Collection)

Through diplomacy and negotiation, President Theodore Roosevelt helped end a war between Russia and Japan in 1905. His accomplishment was recognized the following year when he became the first American to win the prestigious Nobel Peace Prize.

At issue in the Russo-Japanese War was the balance of power in Asia. The Japanese were worried by growing Russian influence, especially in Manchuria and Korea; the Japanese leaders' concern mounted when Russia set up a naval base at Port Arthur (present-day Lushun), China. So, in February, 1904, Japan attacked Port Arthur. Most people expected Russia to win the war that followed, but Japan drove Russia out of Korea and Manchuria and crippled Russia's navy. Then President Roosevelt was asked to arrange a peace conference.

In August, 1905, Roosevelt brought diplomats from Japan and Russia together in Portsmouth, New Hampshire. "I have not an idea whether I can or cannot get peace between Russia and Japan," he wrote a friend. But after weeks of hard work, the Treaty of Portsmouth was signed, ending the war. Roosevelt earned the thanks of world leaders, and the following year was given the Nobel Peace Prize.

Did you know...

Roosevelt's Nobel Peace Prize included an award of almost $37,000. He eventually used the money to aid needy Americans during World War I.

1906

Before 1750

1750-1799

1800-1849

1850-1899

1900-1924

1925-1949

1950-1974

1975-2000

A Year to Remember

1906

President:
Theodore Roosevelt

States:
45

Major events:
San Francisco earthquake; Roosevelt wins Nobel Peace Prize

Illustration: Homeless because of the 1906 earthquake, a San Franciscan family eats dinner outdoors. (Corbis-Bettmann)

In 1906, Americans were enjoying a period of peace and prosperity, and the country was taking its place as an important world power. But the year is best remembered for a devastating natural disaster: the San Francisco earthquake.

Early in the morning on April 18, San Franciscans were awakened by a terrifying rumbling that sent people rushing from their homes. An initial shock and five aftershocks over the next three and one-half hours toppled buildings, split roads, and ruptured gas mains. But the worst damage was caused by fires that raged out of control through the day and into the night. More than 500 people were killed, and another 250,000 were left homeless.

San Franciscans immediately began to rebuild their city. Their determination reflected the spirit of the time. Americans were optimistic and energetic, as was their popular President, Theodore Roosevelt. In November, Roosevelt became the first President to travel abroad while in office: He went to Central America to inspect the Panama Canal, an engineering marvel that was being built by the U.S. That year, he also became the first American to win a Nobel Peace Prize, for negotiating an end to a war between Russia and Japan.

Did you know...

In 1906, Congress passed the Pure Food and Drug Act, regulating the processing of foods and medicines for the first time.

San Francisco Earthquake

One of the most severe earthquakes in U.S. history rocks San Francisco

When:
April 18, 1906

Illustration: Downtown San Francisco after the 1906 earthquake. (EERC/ University of California)

Early on the morning of April 18, 1906, a violent earthquake struck San Francisco. It was followed by an outbreak of fires that lasted three days. About 500 people were killed, 28,000 buildings were destroyed, and 250,000 people were made homeless. This was on of the worst natural disasters that had ever struck the U.S.

The first shock hit at 5:13 a.m. and was followed by five aftershocks in the next three and one-half hours. "The street was gashed in any number of places," wrote one newspaperman. "From some of the holes water was spurting; from others, gas." As the gas ignited, fires spread throughout the city. Because the water mains had ruptured, firefighters were unable to control the flames. Within three days, the business section and many residential areas were in ruins.

Thousands of people fled the city, and tens of thousands were forced to sleep in parks and in refugee camps. But San Franciscans quickly began to rebuild. When San Francisco held the Panama-Pacific International Exposition in 1915, all traces of the earthquake had disappeared. Other earthquakes have hit San Francisco since 1906, but none has been as destructive.

Did you know...

About 6,000 earthquakes are detected around the world every year, but most of them are so minor they do not cause damage.

Before 1750

1750-1799

1800-1849

1850-1899

1900-1924

1925-1949

1950-1974

1975-2000

The Pure Food and Drug Act

The Pure Food and Drug Act

What:
The first federal law to protect American consumers

When:
June 30, 1906

Where:
Washington, D.C.

Illustration: A government inspector at a Chicago packinghouse in 1906. (UPI/Bettmann)

In 1900, Dr. Harvey W. Wiley launched a campaign against harmful foods and unsafe drugs sold in the U.S. Scornful critics labeled him "the chief janitor and policeman of people's insides." But Wiley, a chemist with the U.S. Department of Agriculture, knew what he was talking about. Because there was no government inspection of meat, harmful food was being sold across the country. And patent medicines—usually sold door-to-door without a doctor's prescription—were often laced with dangerous drugs.

Wiley enlisted doctors and women's groups in his crusade to expose the corrupt food and drug industries. His drive got a boost in January, 1906, when Upton Sinclair's novel *The Jungle* was published. In this carefully researched book, Sinclair exposed the deplorable conditions in the meatpacking industry. He revealed that floor sweepings, poi-soned rats, and meat from diseased animals were routinely ground up with meat used to make sausages. On June 30, 1906, Congress passed the Pure Food and Drug Act, the nation's first consumer-protection law. It provided stiff penalties for the manufacture, sale, and transport of foods, drugs, medicines, and liquors that were mislabeled or contained harmful substances.

Did you know...

The Meat Inspection Act, also passed on June 30, 1906, required federal inspection at packing plants and the enforcement of sanitary practices.

The Murder of Stanford White

The murder of Stanford White

What:
Stanford White, a prominent architect, is murdered by the jealous husband of a woman he once romanced

When:
June 25, 1906

Where:
New York City

Illustration: Harry K. Thaw (top center) was the husband of Evelyn Nesbit (inset, left) and the killer of Stanford White (right). (Granger Collection; Brown Bros.)

One June evening in 1906, a lavish party was being held at Madison Square Garden's elegant rooftop restaurant. New York's high society was celebrating the reopening of the Garden, an imposing building that included an arena, a theater, and a ballroom. One of the honored guests was Stanford White, the renowned architect who had designed the building. Suddenly, to the horror of the partygoers, gunshots rang out and White fell dead. He had been shot from behind by Harry K. Thaw, one of the city's wealthiest men.

The handsome, 52-year-old White was a partner in the influential architectural firm of McKim, Mead & White. He had earned fame and wealth designing mansions, churches, office buildings, and public structures such as Manhattan's Washington Square Arch. Though married, White had a reputation for romantic involvements. In 1901, he had been linked to Evelyn Nesbit, a beautiful young showgirl. The relationship had ended when Nesbit married Harry Thaw. But the insanely jealous Thaw believed that his wife was still seeing White, and his jealousy drove him to murder. After the killing, newspapers around the country printed every sordid detail of the "love triangle." Thaw's trial ended with a hung, or deadlocked, jury. But in a second trial, the jury ruled him insane, and he was committed to an asylum.

Did you know...

In addition to buildings, Stanford White designed furniture, jewelry, and magazine covers.

Before 1750

1750-1799

1800-1849

1850-1899

1900-1924

1925-1949

1950-1974

1975-2000

The Great White Fleet

The Great White Fleet

What:
President Theodore Roosevelt sends a fleet of U.S. battleships around the world

When:
Left Virginia on December 16, 1907; returned on February 21, 1909

Illustration: President Theodore Roosevelt welcomes sailors of the Great White Fleet home in 1909. (Theodore Roosevelt Collection, Harvard College Library)

On December 16, 1907, thousands of cheering spectators jammed the shoreline of Hampton Roads, Virginia. They had come to watch 16 snow-white battleships set sail on a historic around-the-world voyage.

The cruise of this Great White Fleet was President Theodore Roosevelt's idea. He believed that the United States should "speak softly, but carry a big stick." He wanted all nations to know that the United States had become a mighty power. Because Japan was acting aggressively in the Pacific, Roosevelt was especially anxious to convince the Japanese that any attack on the Philippine Islands or other American territories would be a serious mistake.

The Great White Fleet's mission was a huge success. The ships and their crews were welcomed enthusiastically everywhere, even in Japan. The impressive display of strength dis-couraged Japan from acting against American interests in the Pacific, and the United States was recognized throughout the world as a major naval power.

Did you know...

The Great White Fleet sailed more than 46,000 miles on its 14–month cruise.

Arts & Entertainment

The Ziegfeld Follies

The Ziegfeld Follies

What:
A series of lavish theatrical revues

Who:
Produced by Florenz Ziegfeld

When:
From 1907 through 1931

Illustration: A fantastic tableau from the 1927 edition of the Ziegfeld Follies. (The Bettmann Archive)

Beautiful women. Gorgeous costumes. Fantastic sets. Hilarious comedians. These were the hallmarks of the Ziegfeld Follies, the annual revues staged by master showman Florenz Ziegfeld. For almost 25 years, beginning in 1907, the glamour and fun of Ziegfeld's shows delighted audiences on Broadway and across the nation.

Ziegfeld started in show business by booking acts for the Chicago World's Fair of 1893. Then he began producing shows himself, and soon developed the mix of glamour, comedy, and music that made his revues hits year after year. Ziegfeld had a sharp eye for talent. Top composers, including Irving Berlin and Jerome Kern, wrote songs for his shows. Among the entertainers who gained fame in his Follies were comedians Fanny Brice, Will Rogers, and W.C. Fields.

Only the best would do for a Ziegfeld revue, and he spared no expense to get it. His showgirls often wore real lace and the latest Paris hats. Stage sets were incredibly elaborate. One number in the 1909 Follies featured 48 showgirls in huge battleship headdresses that had smoke coming out of the smokestacks. Overhead, an actress circled in a mock airplane, scattering roses on the audience.

Did you know...

In addition to the Follies, Florenz Ziegfeld produced *Show Boat*, the great 1927 musical by Jerome Kern and Oscar Hammerstein II.

Before 1750

1750-1799

1800-1849

1850-1899

1900-1924

1925-1949

1950-1974

1975-2000

1908

1908

President:
Theodore Roosevelt

States:
46

Major events:
William Howard Taft elected President;
Henry Ford introduces the Model T

Illustration: An early advertisement for Henry Ford's Model T. (From the collections of Henry Ford Museum and Greenfield Village)

Before 1750

1750-1799

1800-1849

1850-1899

1900-1924

1925-1949

1950-1974

1975-2000

Two midwesterners were the top news-makers of 1908. One was an Ohio man, a portly 300-pound politician who ran successfully for President. The other, from Michigan, was a thin, small-framed engineer with a product that would transform America.

The politician was William Howard Taft, who became the Republican presidential candidate—reluctantly. A lawyer who disliked politics and dreamed of being a Supreme Court justice, Taft was talked into running for President by his friend President Theodore Roosevelt. After Roosevelt decided not to run for reelection in 1908, he arranged for Taft to get the nomination. Promising to continue Roosevelt's policies, Taft won an easy victory over Democrat William Jennings Bryan.

But it was the mechanic from Detroit who had the bigger impact on the American way of life. In 1908, Henry Ford introduced his Model T, a plain but sturdy car built to operate on America's rough roads. Ford wanted to produce a car that everyone—not just the wealthy—could buy. Early models cost $850. But in 1925, Ford was able to reduce the price of the Model T—the most popular car ever built—to $300!

Did you know...

In 1908, a new skyscraper—New York City's Singer Building—soared to the record-breaking height of 45 stories.

60

The Model T Ford

Henry Ford's Model T takes America by storm

Where:
Detroit, Michigan

When:
October, 1908

Illustration: A family proudly poses with its new Model T Ford. (Brown Brothers)

Before 1750

1750-1799

1800-1849

1850-1899

1900-1924

1925-1949

1950-1974

1975-2000

In the early years of the 1900's, only a few rich people could afford a car. After all, automobiles were expensive, unreliable, and sometimes dangerous. Henry Ford had a different idea. He set out to design a car that was inexpensive, reliable, and safe. "I am going to democratize the automobile," he promised. "When I'm through everybody will be able to afford one, and about everybody will have one."

In the fall of 1908, he unveiled the Model T. This plain auto with a four-cylinder engine sold for about $900—a good value, but still more than most people could afford. The Ford company sold about 10,000 the first year. But as people saw how sturdy the Model T was, sales went up, up, and up again. And year after year, the price of the car went down and down! By 1925, it cost only $290. One owner said the Model T was "nimble as a jack rabbit, tough as a hickory stump, simple as a butter churn, unadorned as a farmer's boot."

Henry Ford kept on making Model T's until 1927. The last one built was number 15,456,868. More than half of all cars on the road that year were Model T's. No single car model was ever as popular again.

Did you know...

When the Model T Ford was introduced, it came in six colors. In 1913, there was no color choice. To save money, every Model T was painted black.

The New York- to- Paris Automobile Race of 1908

The New York –to –Paris automobile race of 1908

What:
The most famous of the early long-distance auto races

Where:
From New York City to Paris, France

Who:
Winner driven by George Schuster and Montague Roberts

Illustration: The Thomas Flyer that won the New York– to –Paris Race of 1908. (Bettmann)

In the early 1900's, automobile makers wanted to prove to the public that their "new-fangled machines" were reliable and safe. To show that cars could travel long distances, they promoted a series of international races. The most famous was the New York –to– Paris Race of 1908, known as the Great Race.

On February 12, a quarter of a million spectators cheered as six cars from the U.S., Italy, France, and Germany left New York and headed west. The participants were supposed to drive to Seattle, Washington; take a boat to southern Alaska; drive across Alaska to the Bering Strait; and then sail to Russian Siberia, where the race to Paris would continue. But the German car, a Protos, broke down in Idaho. ("I wish the roads in America were as nice as the people," the driver later said.) After repairs, the Germans drove to Seattle and took a boat directly to Russia. The Americans, in a Thomas Flyer, arrived in Alaska as scheduled, but were unable to proceed because of snow. So they sailed back to Seattle and took a boat to Russia.

Transmission problems further delayed the Americans in Europe, and they arrived in Paris on July 30, four days after the Germans. Nevertheless, the U.S. was declared the winner— because the judges subtracted the week the Americans had spent stuck in Alaska!

Did you know...

Sales of Thomas Flyers jumped 27% as a result of the Great Race victory.

Before 1750

1750-1799

1800-1849

1850-1899

1900-1924

1925-1949

1950-1974

1975-2000

William Howard Taft

William Howard Taft, the 27th President

Born:
September 15, 1857, in Cincinnati, Ohio

Term:
1909–1913

States:
48

Died:
March 8, 1930

Illustration: President William Howard Taft, center, at a parade in New York City in 1910. (Brown Brothers)

William Howard Taft was the only man to serve as both President of the U.S. and Chief Justice of the Supreme Court. He much preferred the Chief Justice's job. "Politics, when I am in it, makes me sick," Taft once wrote.

Taft, a lawyer and a judge, was an imposing man, weighing about 300 pounds. In 1900, he was named to head a commission on the Philippine Islands, which the U.S. had just acquired as a result of the Spanish-American War. He became governor of the Philippines in 1901. President Theodore Roosevelt, his friend, appointed him U.S. Secretary of War in 1904. Four years later, when Roosevelt decided not to run for reelection, he persuaded Taft to run for President. As chief executive, Taft continued many of Roosevelt's policies. But, in time, the friends became opponents. Roosevelt felt that Taft's policies on conservation and tariffs (taxes on imports) favored big business. In 1912, Roo-sevelt opposed him for the Republican nomination. When Taft won it, Roosevelt ran for President on the Progressive, or "Bull Moose," ticket. Thus the Republican vote was split between Taft and Roosevelt, and Woodrow Wilson, a Democrat, won. Taft taught law at Yale University until 1921, when he was named Chief Justice of the Supreme Court, a position he had always wanted. His years on the Court were the happiest of his life.

Did you know...

New Mexico and Arizona became the 47th and 48th states in 1912, during Taft's presidency.

Before 1750

1750-1799

1800-1849

1850-1899

1900-1924

1925-1949

1950-1974

1975-2000

The Founding of the NAACP

Important Events

The founding of the National Association for the Advancement of Colored People, a civil-rights organization

When:
1909

Where:
New York City

Before 1750

1750-1799

1800-1849

1850-1899

1900-1924

1925-1949

1950-1974

1975-2000

Illustration: An NAACP parade in New York City in 1910. (The Bettmann Archive)

In 1908, race riots swept through Springfield, Illinois. For two days, white mobs attacked African-Americans and burned their homes and businesses. Forty-six blacks were killed, including two men who were lynched less than a half mile from Abraham Lincoln's grave. Some 2,000 black men, women, and children fled the city.

Shocked by the terrible riots, 60 black and white leaders met in New York City to discuss how to oppose racism and violence, and gain equality for blacks. They formed the National Negro Committee, which soon changed its name to the National Association for the Advancement of Colored People (NAACP). Among the early leaders was writer and educator W.E.B. DuBois, who edited the organization's magazine *Crisis*.

The NAACP sought to end racial discrimination and violence through a combination of court cases, new laws, and education. In its early days, the organization campaigned especially hard for laws against lynching. In the 1950's and 1960's, the NAACP became a leading force in the civil-rights movement. The oldest civil-rights organization in the U.S., it continues to work for the "elimination of all barriers to political, educational, social, and economic equality."

Did you know...

Among the NAACP's most important court cases was *Brown v. Board of Education of Topeka, Kansas*, the 1954 case that put an end to segregation in public schools.

Robert E. Peary Reaches the North Pole

Illustration: Artic explorer Robert E. Peary with his sled dogs. (Brown Brothers)

Before 1750

1750-1799

1800-1849

1850-1899

1900-1924

1925-1949

1950-1974

1975-2000

"The fame of Columbus," Robert E. Peary once said, "will be equaled only by the man who stands at the top of the world—the discoverer of the North Pole." Peary was determined that he would be the man to achieve that goal.

Peary joined the Navy as a civil engineer in 1881 and developed a consuming curiosity about unexplored, ice-covered Greenland. He led five expeditions there, making many important scientific discoveries. In 1892 he made the dangerous 1,300 mile-journey across northeastern Greenland by dogsled, proving that Greenland was an island.

Peary's first attempt to reach the North Pole was a failure. His feet were so badly frostbitten that he had to have eight toes amputated. His second attempt also failed. For his third effort in the winter of 1908–1909, Peary and his party set up a base camp on Cape Columbia in the Arctic. On March 1, they began the perilous trek northward. Fighting freezing cold, ferocious winds, and sudden openings in the ice, they traveled 400 miles in 37 days. Finally, on the morning of April 6, Peary reached the Pole and planted the American flag in the ice. Later, Peary sent news of his triumph to the world: "Stars and Stripes nailed to the Pole—Peary."

Did you know...

Matthew Alexander Henson, who accompanied Peary on his Arctic expeditions, was the first African-American to reach the North Pole.

Matthew Henson

Matthew Alexander Henson, Arctic explorer

Born:
August 8, 1866, in Charles County, Maryland

Home:
New York City

Died:
March 9, 1955

Illustration: Matthew Henson, a member of the first expedition to reach the North Pole. (The Granger Collection)

When Robert Peary was being hailed for leading the first successful expedition to the North Pole in 1909, no one paid much attention to Matthew Henson. But in reality, Henson had played an essential role in the expedition's dogsled dash to the top of the world. As Peary admitted, "I could not [have done it] . . . without him."

An African-American who was born on a farm in Maryland, Henson left his family and sailed to China as a cabin boy when he was just 14. After a few years at sea, he was working in a hat store in Washington, D.C., when he met Peary, a U.S. Navy officer. Henson soon went to work for Peary and embarked on a lifetime of adventure.

During seven expeditions to the far North with Peary, Henson became a skilled dogsled driver and learned to speak the native Inuit language. On their seventh Arctic trip, in 1909, Peary and Henson set off from Cape Columbia, Canada, to cross the sea ice to the North Pole. After a treacherous journey, during which the temperatures dropped to 40 degrees below zero, the two accomplished their goal. Peary became a national hero, but only years later was Henson's role recognized with a congressional medal and presidential tributes.

Did you know...

A plaque honoring Henson hangs in Maryland's statehouse. And his New York City home is a national historic landmark.

Before 1750

1750-1799

1800-1849

1850-1899

1900-1924

1925-1949

1950-1974

1975-2000

American Troops Sent to Nicaragua

American troops sent to Nicaragua

What:
U.S. Marines quell rebellions and maintain peace in Nicaragua

When:
1909–1933

Illustration: U.S. Marines in Chinenbaga, Nicaragua, in 1913. (Corbis-Bettmann)

Before 1750

1750-1799

1800-1849

1850-1899

1900-1924

1925-1949

1950-1974

1975-2000

In 1909, revolution broke out in the Central American country of Nicaragua. To protect American business interests there—and to help a conservative government take power—President William Howard Taft sent U.S. Marines to Nicaragua. They left when the situation stabilized, but three years later, Nicaraguans opposed to U.S. influence in their country began another rebellion. The Marines returned, and this time they remained, with only short respites, for 20 years.

To quell the 1912 unrest, some 2,600 Marines landed on Nicaragua's west coast as U.S. ships sat offshore. The Americans fought only minor engagements against the rebels and suffered few casualties. But by the end of the year, the revolt was crushed and a pro-American government was in power. A small group of Marines—rarely more than 100—remained in Nicaragua to protect American lives and prop-

erty. The Marines pulled out in 1925, but violence returned to Nicaragua within a few months, and so did the Marines. The Americans trained a national police force and supervised democratic elections, despite opposition from antigovernment rebels. Finally, in 1933, American troops left Nicaragua for good.

Did you know...

A 1916 treaty gave the U.S. the right to build a canal across Nicaragua, similar to the one in Panama. But the second canal was never constructed.

The Founding of the Boy Scouts

Before 1750

1750-1799

1800-1849

1850-1899

1900-1924

1925-1949

1950-1974

1975-2000

Life in America

The Boy Scouts of America are founded

When:
1910

Who:
William D. Boyce, inspired by Robert Baden-Powell

Illustration: Norman Rockwell's painting "Forward America" salutes the Boy Scouts. (© Brown & Bigelow, Inc. & the Boy Scouts of America)

On a visit to London in 1909, Chicago publisher William D. Boyce became lost in a heavy fog. An English Boy Scout helped him find his way. The Scout told Boyce about the Boy Scout movement, founded in England just a year earlier by army officer Robert Baden-Powell. Boyce returned home and founded the Boy Scouts of America in 1910. The new group adopted Baden-Powell's motto, "Be Prepared," and his slogan, "Do a Good Turn Daily."

Today the Boy Scouts of America have almost 4 1/2 million members in five divisions: Cubs, Tigers, Webelos, Scouts, and Explorers. The organization's goal is to improve its members' self-confidence and competence, and to foster leaders and good citizens. The program includes instruction and skill-building in a wide variety of fields, ranging from first aid to ecology. Members earn merit badges for their accomplishments in special fields, and thereby advance in rank through scouting.

Camping and outdoor skills have always been important aspects of scouting. Every four years Boy Scouts from more than 100 nations gather for a giant camp-out known as the International Jamboree.

Did you know...

To become an Eagle Scout, the highest rank in scouting, a young man must have earned at least 21 merit badges.

Lee De Forest and the Radio

Lee De Forest, the father of radio

Born:
August 26, 1873, in Council Bluffs, Iowa

Died:
June 30, 1961

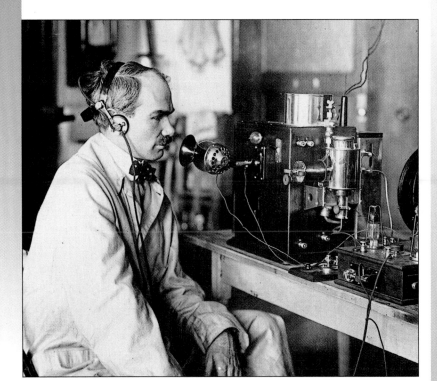

Illustration: Inventor Lee De Forest in a photograph taken in 1907. (The Granger Collection)

On a memorable night in 1910, the voice of the famous tenor Enrico Caruso flowed over the airwaves from the Metropolitan Opera House in New York City. This was the first time a musical radio program had ever been broadcast. And it was made possible by Lee De Forest.

De Forest, known as the "father of radio," was an engineer and inventor who patented more that 300 devices for radio and wireless telegraph communications. His greatest contribution was the invention of the triode in 1906. With the triode it was possible to transmit speech and music over long distances for the first time. This three-element vacuum tube, used for sound amplification or transmission, is basic to such electronic instruments as radio and television.

In 1913, De Forest sold the rights to the triode to the Bell System for $140,000. Others improved on the device that eventually became the basis for transcontinental telephone service, military communications during World War I, and "talking pictures," as well as radio and television. In fact, Lee De Forest laid the groundwork for much of the way we communicate today.

Did you know...

Despite his important inventions, De Forest left an estate of only $1,200 at his death. His businesses were unsuccessful, and he was involved in many lawsuits over patents.

Before 1750

1750-1799

1800-1849

1850-1899

1900-1924

1925-1949

1950-1974

1975-2000

1911

Before 1750

1750-1799

1800-1849

1850-1899

1900-1924

1925-1949

1950-1974

1975-2000

1911

President:
William Howard Taft

States:
46

Major events:
The Triangle Shirtwaist factory fire; the breakup of the oil monopoly; the first cross-country airplane flight

Illustration: Cal Rodgers during his coast-to-coast flight in 1911. (UPI/Bettmann)

In 1911, a terrible fire in a New York factory sparked demands for safer working conditions. Also, the federal government took aim at big business, breaking up the powerful Standard Oil monopoly. And a daring aviator completed the first flight across the country, stopping frequently along the way.

The Triangle Shirtwaist Company's factory in New York City caught fire on March 25. Although the fire blazed for just 30 minutes, 146 people were trapped inside and died. Most of the victims were young immigrant women. Public outrage resulted in stronger health and safety regulations for factories.

In May, the U.S. Supreme Court ordered the huge Standard Oil Company, controlled by John D. Rockefeller, to break into smaller companies. The Court said that Standard Oil's complete control of the oil industry violated the Sherman Antitrust Act. The breakup of Standard Oil

increased competition and ultimately benefited the consumer.

On September 17, pilot Calbraith Rodgers took off in a Burgess-Wright biplane on America's first cross-country flight. A train carrying his wife, mother, mechanics, and spare parts followed him all the way from Sheepshead Bay, New York, to Pasadena, California. The flight took 49 days and required 69 stops (many unscheduled).

Did you know...

Rodgers' actual flying time on his 3,220-mile cross-country trip was 82 hours, 4 minutes.

The Triangle Fire

The Triangle Fire

What:
A fire kills 146 workers, drawing attention to unsafe factories

When:
March 25, 1911

Where:
New York City

Illustration: A fire destroys the Triangle Shirtwaist factory in New York, in 1911. (The Bettmann Archive)

In the early 1900's, immigrants poured into New York City. They took whatever jobs they could find. Many worked long hours at sewing machines in sweatshops, which were often crowded lofts that turned out clothing for the garment industry. One such sweatshop was the Triangle Shirtwaist Company. It occupied the eighth, ninth, and tenth floors of a building in Manhattan.

On March 25, 1911, as 500 of its young women workers were preparing to leave for the day, a fire broke out on the eighth floor. Within minutes, the fire had spread out of control. Workers panicked. Some crowded into freight elevators. Others rushed to the narrow stairwells. There, they found their way blocked—the company had locked most exits to prevent workers from stealing. A single fire escape collapsed under the weight of the fleeing women. Fire trucks rushed to the scene, but their ladders were too short to reach the loft. Horrified bystanders watched as workers, many with their hair and clothing on fire, jumped from the windows to their deaths on the street below. In less than 30 minutes, 146 people were killed. Investigators failed to determine the cause of the fire. But they found many people at fault—the factory owners, the fire department, and city officials. The tragedy drew attention to unsafe factory conditions and helped start a reform movement.

Did you know...

After the fire, New York City passed laws to improve workplace safety.

Before 1750

1750-1799

1800-1849

1850-1899

1900-1924

1925-1949

1950-1974

1975-2000

The Early Days of Airmail

Illustration: A transcontinental airmail flight in 1928. (The Bettmann Archive)

The first experimental airmail delivery in the U.S. took place on Long Island, New York, in the autumn of 1911. Under the direction of the U.S. Postmaster General, pilot Earle Ovington flew six miles from Garden City to Mineola and dropped a bag of mail from the air.

The U.S. Signal Corps attempted a regularly scheduled route in 1918. Its pilots, in training for military duty, were assigned to relay mail from Washington, D.C., to Philadelphia to New York. The first flight from Washington was ill-fated. Its pilot flew in the wrong direction and broke the plane's propeller when he landed south of the capital. Nevertheless, a regular airmail service operated for three months.

After World War I, the Post Office used surplus warplanes to begin coast-to-coast mail service. But lack of navigational aids—there were no aerial maps, lighted runways, or communications systems—made flying at night impossible. So the mail sacks were loaded onto railroad cars each evening. However, by 1924, flight routes were marked by gas beacons spaced three miles apart and airfields were equipped with floodlights. Thus, mail could be flown coast-to-coast in less than 30 hours—three days less than it took by rail.

Did you know...

The first U.S. airmail stamps, printed in 1918, showed a Curtiss "Jenny" flying upside down. Because of this printer's error, the stamps are now priceless collector's items.

Before 1750

1750-1799

1800-1849

1850-1899

1900-1924

1925-1949

1950-1974

1975-2000

Discoveries & Inventions

Glenn Curtiss, pioneer aviator and aircraft designer

Born:
May 21, 1878, in Hammondsport, New York

Died:
July 23, 1930

Glenn Curtiss

Illustration: Glenn Curtiss in June Bug, *one of his early airplanes. (Brown Brothers)*

Seaplanes; bombers; airplanes that take off from ships: Glenn Curtiss envisioned all these advances in aviation and played a key role in bringing them to reality.

Curtiss started off as a bicycle mechanic and manufacturer of motorcycle engines. He first turned to aviation in 1940, when he began making motors for dirigibles. Soon he was designing and producing airplanes. In 1908, his airplane *June Bug* became the first heavier-than-air craft to fly a distance of over half a mile. Three years later, he built the first successful seaplanes. Perhaps his greatest contribution to aviation was the aileron, a hinged wing flap that gave pilots greater control when turning and banking. He was sued by the Wright brothers, who claimed to own the rights to the invention, but the Wrights dropped the suit when Curtiss was awarded the patent for the aileron. In 1911, Curtiss founded the first

American airplane-manufacturing company. That year, he also demonstrated to U.S. Navy officials that planes could land on ships at sea, sparking the development of aircraft carriers. During World War I, his company built thousands of planes for Britain, and Russia, and the U.S. In 1919, one of his Navy-Curtiss "flying boats," the NC-4, made the first transatlantic flight.

Did you know...

Curtiss once pelted a ship with oranges from an airplane to show officials that planes could be used to bomb vessels.

Before 1750

1750-1799

1800-1849

1850-1899

1900-1924

1925-1949

1950-1974

1975-2000

1912

1912

President:
William Howard Taft

States:
48

Major events:
Arizona and New Mexico join the Union; the Titanic sinks at sea; U.S. Marines are sent to Nicaragua; Woodrow Wilson wins the presidential election

Illustration: Boy Scouts raise money to help survivors of the Titanic, *which sank in the North Atlantic. (Corbis-Bettmann)*

Americans welcomed two new states into the Union early in 1912. In January, New Mexico became the 47th state, and Arizona followed a month later. The continental U.S. was complete at last.

International events made headlines that spring and summer. On April 10, the SS *Titanic* embarked on its maiden voyage from England to New York. The elegant ocean liner was supposedly unsinkable. But on April 14, the ship hit an iceberg and went down in the North Atlantic. The *Titanic* lacked enough lifeboats for everyone on board, and more than 1,500 people drowned. Three months later, attention turned to Central America. About 2,700 U.S. Marines were sent to help the Nicaraguan government put down a rebellion.

The presidential election dominated the news in the final months of the year. Republican President William Howard Taft ran for reelection, but he faced stiff competition from Democrat Woodrow Wilson and former President Theodore Roosevelt, also a Republican. Disapproving of Taft's record as President, Roosevelt formed the Progressive "Bull Moose" Party. He promised voters a more progressive government, but in November, Republicans split their votes between Roosevelt and Taft, and Wilson won the election.

Did you know...

At the 1912 Olympic Games in Sweden, Jim Thorpe, a Native American, became the first athlete ever to win gold medals in both the pentathalon and decathalon.

Before 1750

1750-1799

1800-1849

1850-1899

1900-1924

1925-1949

1950-1974

1975-2000

The Sinking of the *Titanic*

The Titanic hits an iceberg and sinks, with 1,500 lives lost

When:
April 14–15, 1912

Where:
Atlantic Ocean, off the coast of Newfoundland, Canada

Illustration: *A painting by Ken Marschall from* The Discovery of the Titanic. *(© Warner/Madison Press Books)*

At noon, on April 10, 1912, the newest, largest, and most luxurious ship in the world steamed majestically out of the harbor of Southampton, England, bound for New York. A British ship, the *Titanic* was making its maiden voyage. Those aboard—2,200 in all—had been told by experts that the ship's double bottom and 16 watertight compartments made it "unsinkable."

By Sunday evening, April 14, news of icebergs nearby reached the *Titanic*. Anxious to make a speed record for the crossing, the captain did not slow down. But lookouts in the crow's nest were alerted to keep an extra-sharp eye. At 11:40, their cry rang out: "Iceberg right ahead!" Just 37 seconds later, the *Titanic* uttered a sickening groan as the iceberg cut a 300-foot gash in its hull. Six watertight compartments were torn open and the cold sea rushed in.

On deck there was pandemonium. There weren't enough lifeboats, and some of them were only half full when they were lowered. At 2:20, a.m., those huddled in the lifeboats watched the *Titanic* nose down and sink into the icy North Atlantic. There were only about 700 survivors.

Did you know...

Legend has it that the *Titanic* band was playing "Nearer My God to Thee" as the ship went down. Actually, it was the hymn *Autumn,* containing the line, "Hold me up in mighty waters."

Before 1750

1750-1799

1800-1849

1850-1899

1900-1924

1925-1949

1950-1974

1975-2000

The Election of 1912

Illustration: The 1912 election pitted Teddy Roosevelt (inset) against President Taft (right) and Woodrow Wilson. (© Chicago Historical Society; inset, Brown Brothers)

When President Theodore Roosevelt decided not to seek reelection in 1908, he chose his friend William Howard Taft as his successor. But after Taft was elected, Roosevelt became increasingly unhappy with Taft's leadership. Roosevelt, a progressive who believed that the federal government should limit the power of huge corporations, believed that Taft had slowed the pace of reform. So in 1912, Roosevelt decided to challenge Taft for the Republican presidential nomination.

Roosevelt was enormously popular, but Taft had the support of Republican leaders and won the nomination. Roosevelt and his backers then formed the Progressive Party, which advocated a federal income tax and voting rights for women, among other reforms. Because Roosevelt had once said that he felt as fit as a bull moose, his new party became known as the "Bull Moose" party. Meanwhile, the Democrats gave their nomination to another reformer, New Jersey governor Woodrow Wilson. Roosevelt, a fiery campaigner, won a larger percentage of the vote—27.4 percent—than any third-party candidate in history and finished ahead of Taft. A fourth candidate, Socialist Eugene V. Debs, took 6 percent of the vote. But the split among the Republicans assured Wilson's election.

Did you know...

At a campaign rally in Wisconsin, a would-be assassin fired a shot at Roosevelt. But the bullet hit his glasses case and a folded-up speech in his pocket, and he wasn't hurt.

Before 1750

1750-1799

1800-1849

1850-1899

1900-1924

1925-1949

1950-1974

1975-2000

The Girl Scouts

The Girl Scouts

What:
An organization that helps girls develop their potential and serve their communities

When:
Founded in 1912

Who:
Founded by Juliette Low

Illustration: During World War I, Girl Scouts collected peach pits. The oil from the pits was used for war industries. (The Bettmann Archive)

Each year, American Girl Scouts ask their friends and neighbors to buy Girl Scout cookies. This fund-raising activity is an annual event for scout troops, which are active all year long. They perform community service, earn badges for various skills and achievements, and participate in activities that help them develop as healthy, productive citizens.

The founder of the American Girl Scouts was Juliette Gordon Low, a Georgian. She was living in Scotland in 1911 when she learned about the British Girl Guides. That organization was headed by Agnes Baden-Powell, sister of Robert Baden-Powell, founder of the Boy Scouts. When Low returned to Savannah in 1912, she founded the American Girl Guides with 18 members. A year later, the group's name changed from Guides to Scouts. Today, there are about three and one-half million Girl Scouts in five age divisions: Daisies, Brownies, Juniors, Cadettes, and Seniors. At each level, the girls are encouraged to develop responsibility, self-confidence, and understanding of themselves and others. Camping is also an important activity. Each summer, thousands of Girl Scouts participate in the "Wyoming Trek," a wilderness camping experience.

Did you know...

The three-leaf clover emblem symbolizes the three parts of the Girl Scout Promise—to serve God and country, to help people at all times, and to live by the Girl Scout Law.

Before 1750

1750-1799

1800-1849

1850-1899

1900-1924

1925-1949

1950-1974

1975-2000

Early Days of Golf

Life in America

Golf becomes a popular sport in the U.S.

When:
First permanent golf clubs established in the 1880's; sport gained wide popularity after 1913

Illustration: American golfers in the 1900's. (© North Wind Pictures)

Golf began in Scotland hundreds of years ago, but it did not begin to interest many Americans until the 1880's. Golf clubs sprang up in Foxburg, Pennsylvania; Yonkers, New York; and elsewhere. And in 1894, these early clubs banded together to form the United States Golf Association (USGA), which established rules for the game and organized official tournaments. The first men's tournament was played at the Newport (Rhode Island) Country Club in 1895.

At first, golf was a game only for the wealthy. But in 1913, a young sporting- goods salesman and former caddy named Francis Ouimet beat the best British golfers in the U.S. Open tournament. Ouimet's surprise victory brought new attention to the sport. Soon there were golfing "duffers" across America, playing on private and public courses. Prizes were offered at major tournaments, and professional golfers could earn a living by competing. Gradually, Americans came to dominate the game. Why did golf become so popular in the United States? Because, said one humorist, it combined "two favorite American pastimes: taking long walks and hitting things with sticks."

Did you know...

Golf was an official event at the 1904 Olympics in St. Louis, Missouri. But it was dropped from later competitions because it was not considered an "ideal" Olympic sport.

Movie serials

What:
Short films that presented thrilling stories in weekly installments

When:
1912 to 1956

Movie Serials

Illustration: Pearl White (left, center) escaped from terrible dangers in many movie serials from 1914 to 1920. (© Pearl White/Photofest)

The movie audience gasps as a mysterious villain called the Wrecker kills the engineer of the world's fastest train. Driverless, the train speeds forward, headed for a disaster. Only the engineer's son can save the lives of the passengers. Will he be able to stop the train? To find out, moviegoers had to come back the following week to see the next episode of *The Hurricane Express*, a 1932 movie serial featuring John Wayne.

Movie serials, which told exciting stories in separate chapters, attracted fans by the millions from 1912 to the 1950's. The most famous serial was *The Perils of Pauline*, which debuted in 1914. As the disaster-prone Pauline, actress Pearl White survived one desperate situation after another for 20 weeks. Each episode ended with a cliff-hanger that made the next installment required viewing. Many of these low-budget tales of high adventure featured heroes

from the comics, such as Dick Tracy and Flash Gordon. Others starred animals, such as Rex "the wonder horse." Today, the special effects in the old serials seem primitive and the plots laughable. In *The Phantom Empire*, for example, cowboy Gene Autry first drives a bunch of rustlers off his land in the American West, and then battles unearthly warriors from an underground empire. In 1935, that unlikely tale kept fans on the edge of their seats.

Did you know...

Television series replaced movie serials in fans' affections in the 1950's.

Before 1750

1750–1799

1800–1849

1850–1899

1900–1924

1925–1949

1950–1974

1975–2000

The Ashcan School

The Ashcan School

What:
A group of realist painters, led by Robert Henri

Where:
New York City

When:
Late nineteenth and early twentieth centuries

Illustration: "Backyard Greenwich Village," a 1914 painting by John Sloan. (© 1966: Whitney Museum of American Art, New York)

In art, the term "school" usually refers to a group of artists who work in a similar style. But the painters of the so-called Ashcan School were even more closely bound than that. They all studied under the same teacher, Robert Henri, and were greatly influenced by him.

Henri was an Ohio-born artist who painted mainly portraits. He used strong colors and sharp contrasts of light and dark—executed with loose, quickly applied brush strokes—to create a lively overall impression rather than a realistic study. He never flattered his subjects, but tried to catch them "to the life." His students—John Sloan, Everett Shinn, William Glackens, George Luks, and George Bellows—used the same spontaneous style to portray real life in New York City in the late nineteenth and early twentieth centuries. They were called the Ashcan School because there was no aspect of city life they wouldn't paint, including the grimy alleys where ashcans were kept. Each artist had his own special interests. Sloan favored bustling street scenes. Shinn loved the theater and circuses. Luks painted colorful characters and the down-and-out, while Bellows often depicted sporting events, especially boxing matches. But the real subject for all the Ashcan School painters was the diverse, vital city itself.

Did you know...

George Bellows was a talented athlete. He gave up the chance to become a professional baseball player when he became a serious art student.

Before 1750

1750-1799

1800-1849

1850-1899

1900-1924

1925-1949

1950-1974

1975-2000

Notable People

Thomas Woodrow Wilson, the 28th President of the United States

Born:
December 28, 1856, in Staunton, Virginia

Term:
1913–1921

Died:
February 3, 1924

Illustration: Woodrow Wilson, the 28th President. (The White House Historical Association, National Geographic Society)

Woodrow Wilson

Woodrow Wilson was a firm believer in peace, but he led the country into World War I. After the war, he campaigned tirelessly for a just peace and a world organization. But his hopes were frustrated, and illness cast a shadow over his last years as President.

In his first term, Wilson helped reform the banking system and pass a law prohibiting child labor. In 1914, when war began in Europe, he believed America should remain neutral. In fact, he was reelected in 1916 on the slogan "He kept us out of war." But by the spring of 1917, German submarines were attacking American ships and forced Wilson into war. Thousands of American soldiers were soon fighting in Europe.

When allied forces defeated Germany in 1918, Wilson attended the peace conference at Versailles in France. He wanted a fair peace, but the French and British insisted on the harsh punishment of Germany. Wilson fought hard for the establishment of the League of Nations, which he believed would help keep peace. Yet although the League was formed, the U.S. Senate refused to allow America to join. In 1919, when Wilson was on a tour to promote support for the League, he suffered a stroke. He remained as President until March, 1921, but he was never again well enough to provide strong leadership.

Did you know...

Before his presidency, Wilson was president of Princeton University and Governor of New Jersey.

Before 1750

1750-1799

1800-1849

1850-1899

1900-1924

1925-1949

1950-1974

1975-2000

The Income Tax Becomes Legal

Before 1750

1750-1799

1800-1849

1850-1899

1900-1924

1925-1949

1950-1974

1975-2000

The income tax becomes legal

What:
The 16th Amendment to the U.S. Constitution is ratified, allowing the government to collect taxes on income

When:
February 25, 1913

Illustration: An 1895 cartoon shows Uncle Sam collecting income taxes from famous millionaires. (Corbis-Bettmann)

Every spring, Americans pull out their calculators and wade through a year's worth of receipts, trying to figure what they owe the government before the April 15 deadline. Filing an income-tax return—and complaining about it—is an American ritual.

The U.S. government collected its first income tax in 1862 to help pay for the Civil War. That tax ended in 1872. The government passed another income-tax law in 1894, but the Supreme Court found the tax unconstitutional. It wasn't until the states ratified the 16th Amendment to the Constitution in 1913 that the government's right to collect an income tax was established. At first, very few people were affected. Only those making more than $3,000—a mere 1 percent of workers—had to pay a tax. The highest rate at that time was 7 percent, on incomes of more than $500,000.

Today, the Internal Revenue Service, the nation's tax collector, processes more than 100 million tax returns each year. Personal and corporate income taxes are the government's major source of revenue. The income tax is often hotly debated in Congress and during election campaigns, but no one has yet proved that there is a better way to collect enough money to keep the government running.

Did you know...

The first tax law was about 14 pages long. Today, after many changes, the U.S. Tax Code fills many thousands of pages.

The Armory Show

The Armory Show

What:
An exhibit of modern art that shocked Americans

Where:
New York City

When:
1913

Illustration: One of Marcel Duchamp's Armory Show paintings, (Philadelphia Museum of Art: Louise and Walter Annenberg Collection)

Art lovers were outraged. Critics were appalled. The exhibit that opened at the 69th Regiment Armory in New York City in February, 1913, sent shock waves through the art world. Some 1,500 paintings and sculptures were displayed in the show, and many of them were unlike anything Americans had seen before.

The International Exposition of Modern Art, better known today as the Armory Show, introduced the works of modern American artists such as Maurice Prendergast and John Sloan. But the organizers also included about 500 works by modern European painters, including Pablo Picasso, Henri Matisse, and Paul Cézanne. The European works gave many Americans their first introduction to Cubism, Expressionism, and other new trends in art. Modern American works seemed tame in comparison. Critics called the European painters

"madmen" and scoffed at their works, because they did not attempt to show people and objects as they really looked. One critic said that a now-famous work by the Cubist painter Marcel Duchamp, "Nude Descending a Staircase," looked like "an explosion in a shingle factory." But the Armory Show influenced a generation of artists and opened a new era in American art.

Did you know...

Despite the hostility that greeted the Armory Show, 250,000 people went to see it during its monthlong run.

Before 1750

1750-1799

1800-1849

1850-1899

1900-1924

1925-1949

1950-1974

1975-2000

Refrigerators

Judge *value* by these things...

simplicity
· ·
economy of
operation
· ·
quietness
· ·
roominess
· ·
the opinion of
fifty thousand
discriminating
users

THE General Electric Refrigerator is so simple that it hasn't a single exposed moving part. It hasn't a belt or a fan or a drain-pipe. It has no connections or stuffing boxes. It never needs oiling because the hermetically sealed casing which holds *all* the mechanism also holds a permanent supply of oil.

Refrigerators

What:
Mechanical devices for cooling food

When:
Cold-air process of refrigeration invented in 1842; first household refrigerator introduced in 1913

Who:
First air-cooling machine invented by John Gorrie

Where:
Apalachicola, Florida

Illustration: An advertisement for a new refrigerator in a 1928 magazine. (Friday Associates International)

Today, Americans take the refrigerator for granted. But until 1913, keeping food and drinks cool and fresh was much more difficult.

The father of modern refrigeration was John Gorrie, a Florida doctor. Because his patients suffered terribly from the Florida heat, Gorrie built an air-cooling machine in 1842. It compressed air, cooled it in a cold-water bath, then cooled the air further by quickly decompressing it. Gorrie realized that his process could also be used for refrigeration and ice making, so he patented his invention for cooling air, but he couldn't find anyone willing to manufacture it.

It wasn't until the 1870's that mechanical cooling machines were manufactured. Then, businessmen were able to build ice-making plants in major cities. For more than 50 years, homemakers kept perishable foods in insulated iceboxes, with a new block of ice being delivered every few days by an iceman. By 1910, refrigeration machines had become much smaller, and many homes in cities had electricity. Finally, in 1913, a Chicago company manufactured the first household refrigerator, the "Domelre," an abbreviation of *domestic electric* refrigerator.

Did you know...

In 1916, Frigidaire offered its first refrigerators. The company's slogan in the 1920's was "No one has to stay home [to wait for the iceman] when you have a Frigidaire!"

Before 1750

1750-1799

1800-1849

1850-1899

1900-1924

1925-1949

1950-1974

1975-2000

1914

1914

President:
Woodrow Wilson

States:
48

Major events:
World War I begins in Europe; Panama Canal opens

Illustration: A ship travels through the newly opened Panama Canal. (© Alexander Alland, Sr./Corbis-Bettmann)

As 1914 began, Americans were looking forward to a period of growing prosperity. But events at home and abroad during the year greatly reduced the country's optimism.

In April, trouble came in Mexico. The crew of a U.S. Navy ship was briefly taken captive in the Mexican port of Tampico, and the navy reacted by bombarding and occupying the city of Veracruz. A war seemed possible, but diplomats finally reached a negotiated settlement. That same month, violence broke out near Ludlow, Colorado. On April 20, security forces of a huge mining company fired on striking miners and burned down their tent city. Two women and 11 children died. The angry miners took up arms and blew up mine entrances. President Woodrow Wilson sent troops to restore peace, but the battle between business and workingmen troubled the nation.

That summer, Americans took pride in the opening of the Panama Canal, which connected the Atlantic and Pacific oceans and promised to increase U.S. trade and influence. But the event was overshadowed by the outbreak of World War I in Europe. The assassination of the heir to the throne of Austria-Hungary led to a chain of events that caused two great blocs of nations to declare war on each other. The war cast a cloud over America, which would eventually be drawn into the conflict.

Did you know...

The Wrigley Company introduced Doublemint chewing gum in 1914.

Before 1750

1750-1799

1800-1849

1850-1899

1900-1924

1925-1949

1950-1974

1975-2000

Opening of the Panama Canal

Before 1750

1750-1799

1800-1849

1850-1899

1900-1924

1925-1949

1950-1974

1975-2000

Important Events

The Panama Canal opens a pathway between the Atlantic and Pacific oceans

When:
August 15, 1914

Where:
the Isthmus of Panama in Central America

Illustration: The construction of the Panama Canal. (The Granger Collection)

The Panama Canal has been called the greatest engineering feat of the modern age. It cuts the travel distance from the Atlantic to the Pacific for ships by fully 7,000 miles.

A canal, to be dug through a 51-mile neck of land in Panama, had long been a dream. In fact, a French company had tried to build it in the 1880s but had failed. President Theodore Roosevelt revived the dream in 1903 when he arranged with Panama for the United States to build the canal. In 1904, the digging began. For the next 10 years, 50 to 60 giant steam shovels gouged out 200 trainloads of earth each day. Over 40,000 workers struggled against 120-degree heat, repeated landslides, accidents with dynamite, and the challenges of building six pairs of monstrous canal locks. Some 6,000 workers died during the construction.

In late 1913, the digging ended at last. The next year, the Panama Canal opened as the S.S. *Ancon* made the first passage through it. A voyage that had once taken weeks or even months now took just seven or eight hours. The cost of construction? Nearly $350 million spent by the U.S., in addition to $285 million spent by the French—about $7 billion in today's money.

Did you know...

Although most people think the Panama Canal goes in an east-west direction, it actually goes northwest to southeast as the map shows.

The Ludlow Massacre

The Ludlow Massacre

What:
A violent clash in the struggle for worker rights

Where:
Ludlow, Colorado

When:
April 20, 1914

Illustration: Colorado militiamen look down on the striking miners' tent village at Ludlow, Colorado. (Colorado Historical Society)

In 1913, the miners at the Colorado Fuel and Iron Company demanded better treatment from their employer. The miners worked 12-hour days in dangerous conditions. They paid high rents to live in company-owned housing and had to buy food at expensive, company-owned stores. They wanted safer conditions, higher pay, and the right to join a union. In October, when the company flatly refused all their demands, 9,000 workers went on strike. Evicted from company housing, they moved to makeshift tent cities. Soon the Colorado state militia arrived to keep order.

The standoff lasted through the winter. Then, on April 20, 1914, members of the militia claimed that shots were being fired at them by miners in the tent city at Ludlow, Colorado. The militia responded by raking the tent city with machine-gun fire. Then they splashed kerosene over the tents and set them afire. At least 20 people, including 11 children and two women, were killed in the action, which came to be known as the Ludlow Massacre. The mine workers retreated to the mountains with guns and explosives. In the next few weeks, more than 100 people on both sides were killed. The nation was horrified, but the company continued to resist the workers' demands.

Did you know...

Colorado Fuel and Iron was owned by John D. Rockefeller, who visited the region in 1915 and ordered improvement of the miners' living and working conditions.

Before 1750

1750-1799

1800-1849

1850-1899

1900-1924

1925-1949

1950-1974

1975-2000

The Passenger Pigeon

Before 1750

1750-1799

1800-1849

1850-1899

1900-1924

1925-1949

1950-1974

1975-2000

Life in America

The passenger pigeon

What:
A once common bird, now extinct

Where:
Eastern North America

When:
Last known passenger pigeon died in 1914

Illustration: Millions of passenger pigeons flourished in the U.S. in the 1800's. (Grand Rapids Art Museum, gift of Ruth Skwarek)

In 1813, naturalist John James Audubon was amazed to see a mile-wide flock of birds that took three days to pass overhead. Daylight, he wrote, "was obscured as if by an eclipse." The migratory birds were passenger pigeons, the most numerous species in North America at the time. But 101 years later, not a single passenger pigeon could be found. Hunters and settlers had driven the species to extinction.

The passenger pigeon was a beautiful bird, about 17 inches long, with a blue-gray head and neck, wine-colored throat and breast, and red feet. Scientists think there were once more than three billion of them. They gathered in flocks and nesting colonies numbering tens of millions. When they roosted in a tree, their combined weight could break branches. Native Americans and early settlers hunted the birds for food. But by the 1850's, commercial hunters were killing millions of the birds and shipping them to market. Meanwhile, settlers were moving west, cutting down the oak and beech forests where the pigeons nested. By 1900, no passenger pigeons could be found in the wild, and only a few flocks remained in captivity. When the last bird died on September 1, 1914, at the Cincinnati Zoo, the species disappeared forever.

Did you know...

The last known passenger pigeon was a female named Martha, for Martha Washington. Its body is on display at the National Museum of Natural History in Washington, D.C.

Important Events

The Sinking of the *Lusitania*

The British passenger ship *Lusitania* is sunk by a German submarine during World War I

Where:
Off the coast of Ireland

When:
May 7, 1915

Illustration: *The* Lusitania *sinks after being hit by a German torpedo. (Mary Evans Picture Library/Photo Researchers)*

On May 2, 1915, the British ocean liner *Lusitania* steamed out of New York Harbor bound for Liverpool, England. World War I had been raging in Europe for nine months, pitting Britain and its allies against Germany and its allies. German submarines prowled the ocean in search of British ships, so transatlantic crossings were very dangerous. Yet 1,959 people were aboard the *Lusitania*, including 197 Americans.

By May 7, the *Lusitania* was off the coast of Ireland. Suddenly, at 2:15 p.m., a German submarine fired a torpedo and hit the liner amidships. The liner shuddered with the explosion and listed sharply to one side, making it hard to lower lifeboats. In 18 minutes, the *Lusitania* was gone. So were all but 761 of those aboard.

Germany claimed that the liner was carrying armaments. Britain denied this, saying that only a small store of rifle ammunition had been on board. The attack on innocent passengers was condemned by President Woodrow Wilson. The sinking of the *Lusitania* heightened tensions between the German and U.S. governments and caused a wave of anti-German feeling in America. But the U.S. did not enter the war against Germany until 1917.

Did you know...

The *Lusitania*'s captain had been told to take a zigzag course to avoid German submarines off Ireland. For unknown reasons, he failed to do so.

Before 1750

1750-1799

1800-1849

1850-1899

1900-1924

1925-1949

1950-1974

1975-2000

Pershing Chases Pancho Villa

Before 1750

1750-1799

1800-1849

1850-1899

1900-1924

1925-1949

1950-1974

1975-2000

Important Events

Pershing chases Pancho Villa

What:
General John J. Pershing pursues Mexican bandit Pancho Villa

When:
March 1916 to February 1917

Where:
Mexico

Illustration: General Pershing crosses the Rio Grande in pursuit of Pancho Villa in 1916. (The Bettmann Archive)

From 1910 to 1920, revolution and civil war swept through Mexico. The turmoil spilled over the U.S. border several times, but the worst incident occurred on March 9, 1916. Mexican raiders attacked Columbus, New Mexico, robbing a bank and killing 17 people. Immediately, General John J. Pershing was ordered to lead U.S. Army units across the border into Mexico. His mission was to disperse the raiders and capture their leader, Pancho (Francisco) Villa, a Mexican bandit and revolutionary who was legendary for boldness.

For months, Pershing's men chased Villa through northern Mexico. The Americans clambered over mountains, suffered through hot dry days and cold nights, and ran out of supplies. They killed or scattered most of the bandits, but Villa himself was always a step ahead of them.

The Mexican government ignored the Per-

shing expedition at first. But as the Americans pushed south, they clashed with Mexican troops, and Mexico protested to President Woodrow Wilson. Unwilling to risk war, Wilson ordered Pershing to return to the U.S. in February, 1917. Pancho Villa remained free, and his escape from Pershing made him an even greater hero to many Mexicans.

Did you know...

One of Pershing's lieutenants pursuing Villa was George Patton, who became a famous general in World War II.

The Lafayette Escadrille

The Lafayette Escadrille

What:
A squadron of American pilots fighting for the French in World War I

Where:
France

When:
1916–1918

Illustration: Pilots of the Lafayette Escadrille, a squadron of Americans fighting for France in World War I.

"This war will perhaps be my death, but in spite of it all, I owe it a profound gratitude." The young man who wrote those words in his diary, James McConnell, was one of a daring group of American pilots who fought for France early in World War I.

When the war broke out in 1914, the U.S. at first declared neutrality. But many Americans went off to fight for Britain and France against Germany. Some became pilots in the French army. In April, 1916, they convinced the French to create an all-American squadron—the Lafayette Escadrille. The squadron became famous for the bravery, skill, and high spirits of its pilots, who kept two lion cubs ("Whiskey" and "Soda") as mascots.

In their Nieuport and Spad biplanes, Lafayette Escadrille pilots shot down 199 German planes. Raoul Lufbery, the squadron's ace, downed 17. But the cost was high: The squadron lost almost a third of its pilots, including Lufbery and McConnell. In 1918, after the United States entered the war, most of the Lafayette Escadrille pilots joined the U.S. Air Service.

Did you know...

The Lafayette Escadrille was named for the Marquis de Lafayette, the French hero of the American Revolution.

Before 1750

1750-1799

1800-1849

1850-1899

1900-1924

1925-1949

1950-1974

1975-2000

1917

A Year to Remember

1917

States:
48

Major event:
United States enters World War I on the side of the Allied Powers, fighting against Germany and Austria-Hungary

Illustration: A parade of new soldiers marches up New York City's Fifth Avenue in 1917, soon after the U.S. entry into World War I. (The Bettmann Archive)

"He kept us out of war." That slogan helped Woodrow Wilson win a second term as President in November, 1916. Most Americans wanted the U. S. to stay out of World War I, which had been raging in Europe for two years. But in April, 1917, only a month after Wilson's second inauguration, the nation entered the conflict.

In theory, the U.S. had been neutral in the war between the Allied Powers (France, Britain, Italy, and Russia) and the Central Powers (Germany and Austria-Hungary). In reality, America had been providing support to the Allies in the form of money and supplies. In retaliation, German submarines began attacking U.S. and Allied merchant ships crossing the Atlantic. The attacks reached a peak early in 1917, with four American ships sunk in March alone. Realizing that the U.S. could no longer remain neutral, Wilson asked Congress, on April 2, to declare war.

The U.S. acted quickly to raise taxes and sell bonds to pay for the war effort. Millions of men were drafted into service. By October, the first American troops had reached the front in France. Their arrival ensured an eventual victory for the Allies.

Did you know...

In 1917, the U.S. acquired the Virgin Islands (St. Thomas, St. John, and St. Croix) from Denmark. The $25 million purchase kept Germany from establishing a naval base there and threatening the Panama Canal.

92

Ocean Liners

Before 1750

1750-1799

1800-1849

1850-1899

1900-1924

1925-1949

1950-1974

1975-2000

Ocean liners

What:
"Floating Palaces" carry passengers in luxury and style

When:
Peak years, 1900–1940

Where:
North Atlantic, between the United States and Europe

Illustration: An ocean liner departs from New York in the 1930's. (FPG International)

You spend the day soaking up the sun, swimming in the pool, and playing shuffleboard. Then you join friends in the "Garden Lounge," where tea is served among towering palm trees and Greek statues. After changing into formal clothes in your stateroom, you make your way along thickly carpeted corridors to the main dining room, where you have been invited to be a guest at the captain's table. After a superb dinner, you dance to the romantic music of the ship's orchestra.

No form of transportation has ever been more glamorous than the ocean liners that carried passengers between the U.S. and Europe. The heyday of these "floating palaces" was from 1900 to 1940. Aboard such ships as the *Aquitania* (which carried 4,000 passengers), the *Normandie*, and the *Queen Elizabeth*, those who could afford the passage were treated like royalty. In 1912, the *Titanic* hit an iceberg and sank, killing 1,500 people. But on most crossings, seasickness was the only peril. During World War II, many of the huge liners were used as troop transports. After the war, new ships like the *United States* kept transatlantic service alive. But gradually jet aircraft, which were faster and cheaper, replaced the queens of the sea. Today, ocean liners are used mainly for pleasure cruises.

Did you know...

In 1952, the *United States* won an award for the fastest ocean crossing: 3 days, 10 hours, and 40 minutes from New York to England.

Luxury Train Travel

Illustration: The luxurious parlor car on a pre–World War II passenger train. (FPG International)

Twentieth Century Limited. Super Chief. Broadway Limited. Rio Grande Zephyr. In the first half of the twentieth century, those names meant glamour, romance, even intrigue and mystery. They were famous passenger trains—the quickest, most comfortable, and most fashionable way to travel.

During the first half of the nineteenth century, traveling by train meant spending hours, even days, on hard wooden benches and often breathing in billows of coal smoke that flew in the open windows. But in 1865, George Pullman revolutionized railroad service when he introduced his famous sleeping cars. Soon, passengers were riding on plush seats that converted to comfortable sleeping berths at night. By the 1880's, trains, as one passenger wrote, were "traveling palaces."

By the early 1900's, railroads were offering everything from maid service to haircuts. Dining cars served gourmet meals with fine linens, crystal, and expensive china. Afterwards, passengers withdrew to observation lounges to enjoy the scenery as their trains zipped along smooth tracks. Luxury trains between New York, Chicago, and Los Angeles were celebrated in plays, songs, and movies. But after World War II, travelers chose speed over glamour and abandoned railroads for airplanes.

Did you know...

To lure passengers from the rival Broadway Limited, the Twentieth Century Limited refunded each passenger a dollar for each hour the train was late.

Before 1750

1750-1799

1800-1849

1850-1899

1900-1924

1925-1949

1950-1974

1975-2000

The Zimmermann Telegram

The Zimmermann Telegram

What:
A secret telegram proposing a joint German-Mexican attack on the U.S.

When:
January 16, 1917

Illustration: A cartoon from 1917 shows a German offering a Mexican U.S. territory in exchange for a military partnership. (American History Magazine / Cowles Communications)

On January 16, 1917, German foreign secretary Arthur Zimmermann sent a secret telegram to Johann von Bernstorff, the German ambassador to the U.S. In the telegram, Zimmermann told of a plan to form a military alliance with Mexico if the U.S. entered World War I. This plan called for a German-Mexican joint attack on the U.S. If the two were victorious, Mexico would regain its "lost territory" of Texas, New Mexico, and Arizona. But British agents intercepted and decoded the telegram, and sent a copy to President Woodrow Wilson.

Wilson had been reelected the previous November, largely because of his neutral stance on the war, which had been raging through Europe since 1914. He hoped that peace would come through negotiations. But when the German government made no attempt to deny the Zimmermann Telegram, Wilson realized that Germany had no intention of ending the war peacefully. On March 1, Wilson released the text of the telegram to the press. Angry over German plans to attack the U.S., Americans began to support U.S. entry into World War I. Their resolve strengthened after German submarines sank several American cargo ships. On April 6, 1917, three months after interception of the telegram, the U.S. declared war on Germany.

Did you know...

Mexico rejected Germany's offer to attack the U.S. and remained neutral throughout World War I.

Before 1750

1750-1799

1800-1849

1850-1899

1900-1924

1925-1949

1950-1974

1975-2000

The U.S. Buys the Virgin Islands

Before 1750

1750-1799

1800-1849

1850-1899

1900-1924

1925-1949

1950-1974

1975-2000

The U.S. buys the Virgin Islands

What:
$25 million purchase of three islands from Denmark

Where:
Saint Thomas, Saint Croix, and Saint John in the Caribbean Sea

When:
Transferred on March 31, 1917

Illustration: Danish and American troops gather on Saint Thomas in 1917 for the transfer of the Virgin Islands. (Dept of Conservation & Cultural Affairs/Government of the Virgin Islands)

In 1917, the U.S. bought the Danish West Indies from Denmark for $25 million. It was the most expensive land purchase the U.S. government had ever made, yet it transferred a mere 136 square miles of land. Now known as the U.S. Virgin Islands, the territory includes the islands of Saint Thomas, Saint Croix, and Saint John, and about 50 small islets.

Three years before the purchase, World War I began in Europe and the U.S completed work on the Panama Canal. President Woodrow Wilson feared that Germany, which was at war with Denmark, might try to take control of the Danish West Indies. If successful, the powerful German navy would have a deepwater harbor in the Caribbean Sea from which it could attack the Canal. Wilson decided to buy the islands to protect America's $350 million Canal investment.

In August, 1916, U.S. Secretary of State Robert Lansing and Ambassador Constantin Brun of Denmark concluded a treaty for the sale of the islands. The formal transfer took place on March 31, 1917, as troops from both countries watched the Stars and Stripes replace the Danish flag on Saint Thomas.

Did you know...

In 1917, the major business of the Virgin Islands was the export of sugar and rum. Today, the chief industry is tourism.

Years to Remember

1492 **1**:15	1755 **1**:74	1803 **2**:61	1850 **3**:57	1883 **4**:79	1917 **5**:92	1942 **7**:5	1962 **8**:21	1981 **8**:91
1541 **1**:26	1765 **1**:81	1812 **2**:70	1852 **3**:62	1886 **4**:85	1918 **6**:5	1943 **7**:21	1963 **8**:28	1984 **9**:8
1587 **1**:34	1773 **1**:86	1814 **2**:74	1859 **3**:73	1890 **4**:95	1920 **6**:21	1944 **7**:33	1967 **8**:44	1987 **9**:13
1619 **1**:42	1775 **1**:88	1819 **2**:80	1860 **3**:78	1893 **5**:9	1923 **6**:32	1945 **7**:44	1968 **8**:47	1989 **9**:15
1620 **1**:44	1776 **2**:5	1825 **2**:89	1861 **3**:80	1898 **5**:27	1927 **6**:44	1948 **7**:65	1969 **8**:53	1990 **9**:19
1630 **1**:49	1777 **2**:16	1829 **3**:5	1862 **3**:86	1901 **5**:43	1929 **6**:50	1950 **7**:73	1970 **8**:59	1991 **9**:21
1676 **1**:55	1778 **2**:21	1836 **3**:16	1863 **4**:5	1904 **5**:51	1933 **6**:67	1951 **7**:76	1972 **8**:66	1992 **9**:23
1682 **1**:58	1781 **2**:25	1844 **3**:35	1864 **4**:18	1906 **5**:54	1935 **6**:73	1952 **7**:81	1973 **8**:69	1994 **9**:34
1692 **1**:61	1787 **2**:32	1846 **3**:43	1865 **4**:27	1908 **5**:60	1937 **6**:79	1956 **7**:90	1974 **8**:73	1995 **9**:37
1718 **1**:66	1789 **2**:37	1847 **3**:48	1868 **4**:39	1911 **5**:71	1939 **6**:85	1957 **7**:92	1976 **8**:77	1996 **9**:53
1729 **1**:68	1793 **2**:45	1848 **3**:53	1871 **4**:54	1912 **5**:74	1941 **6**:90	1958 **7**:95	1980 **8**:88	1997 **9**:68
1735 **1**:71	1801 **2**:55	1849 **3**:55	1876 **4**:62	1914 **5**:85				

A

abolition **2**:90; **3**:21, 23, 62, 68, 73
abortion, legalization of **8**:69
Academy Awards
  Casablanca **7**:19
  Citizen Kane **6**:95
  Cooper, Gary **6**:14
  Gone With the Wind **6**:87
  Titanic **9**:86
Acadians **1**:74
Acoma pueblo **1**:23
Adams, Abigail **2**:52, 53
Adams, John **2**:49
  Alien and Sedition Acts **2**:51
  Continental Congress, First **1**:87
  died on 50th anniversary of
    Declaration of Independence
    2:56
  E Pluribus Unum **2**:5
  Paris, Treaty of **2**:29
  Washington (D.C.) **2**:52
  White House **2**:53
Adams, John Quincy **2**:89, 90; **3**:16
  Adams, John **2**:49
  Amistad case **3**:28
  Monroe Doctrine **2**:88
Adams, Samuel **1**:80, 84, 85, 86, 89
Adams-Onís Treaty **2**:82
adding machines **5**:11
Adventures of Huckleberry Finn **4**:83
advertising
  air conditioners **5**:47
  barbed wire **4**:58
  Colt revolver **3**:20
  Gillette razor **5**:20
  McCormick Reaper **3**:15
  Model T Ford **5**:60
  refrigerators **5**:84
aerodrome **5**:25
Africa
  Clinton, Bill, visit by **9**:92
  North Africa, invasion of **7**:14
  slave trade **2**:65
  Somalia, U.S. troops in **9**:27
  triangular slave trade **1**:64
African-Americans
  Amistad case **3**:28
  Anderson, Marian **6**:85
  arson destruction of
    African-American churches
    9:52
  Attucks, Crispus **1**:84
  Brown v. *Board of Education* **7**:87
  Chamberlain, Wilt **8**:22
  civil-rights sit-ins **8**:9
  Cosby Show, The **9**:10
  desegregation of the armed forces
    7:67; **9**:87
  Detroit riots (1967) **8**:44
  draft riots (1863) **4**:13
  Estéban **1**:22
  Evers, Medgar **8**:30
  54th Massachusetts Regiment
    4:12
  first captive Africans brought to
    Virginia **1**:43
  Fugitive Slave Act **3**:59
  Harlem Renaissance **6**:36
  Henson, Matthew **5**:66
  Johnson, Henry **6**:7
  King, Martin Luther, Jr. **8**:50
  King, Rodney **9**:23

  Little Rock school integration **7**:92,
    93
  Los Angeles riots (1992) **9**:24
  march on Washington **8**:31
  McDaniel, Hattie **6**:87
  Medal of Honor **9**:70
  Meredith, James **8**:24
  "Million Man March" **9**:37, 50
  Montgomery bus boycott **7**:89
  NAACP **5**:64
  New Orleans, Battle of **2**:76
  Oberlin College **3**:13
  Plessy v. *Ferguson* **5**:22
  Porgy and Bess **6**:74
  Powell, Colin **9**:46
  Robinson, Jackie **7**:60
  Roots **8**:81
  Scott, Dred **3**:70
  Scottsboro case **6**:60
  Selma-to-Montgomery marches
    8:37
  Simpson, O.J., trials **9**:40, 65
  Spanish-American War **5**:28
  Turner, Nat **3**:11
  Tuskegee airmen **7**:9
  Underground Railroad **3**:21
  Vesey, Denmark **2**:84
  Wilder, Douglas **9**:15
  Williams, Daniel Hale **5**:9
aging and aged **8**:40
Agnew, Spiro T. **8**:69, 74
agriculture
  Deere's steel plow **3**:26
  Dust Bowl **6**:57
  Granger movement **4**:61
  McCormick Reaper **3**:15
  plantations **2**:60
  Shakers were first to sell garden
    seeds by mail **3**:46
  victory gardens **7**:18
Aguinaldo, Emilio **5**:31
Ahab (fictional character) **3**:61
aileron **6**:73
air conditioners **5**:47
aircraft carriers **5**:73; **7**:13
Air Force, U.S. **7**:61
  B-2 stealth bomber **9**:33
  Davis, Benjamin O. **7**:9
  O'Grady, Scott **9**:43
  Saudi Arabian bombing of U.S.
    troops **9**:58
  Strategic Air Command **7**:58
  see also Army Air Forces, U.S.
airmail, early days of **5**:72; **6**:5
airplanes *see* aviation
Alabama
  1819 **2**:80
  Horseshoe Bend National Military
    Park **2**:75
  Montgomery bus boycott **7**:89
  Natchez Trace National Parkway
    2:59
  Scottsboro case **6**:60
  Selma-to-Montgomery marches
    8:37
  tornadoes (1998) **9**:94
Alabama (warship) **4**:23
Alamo **1**:66, 70; **3**:16, 17
Alamogordo (New Mexico) **7**:52
Alaska **3**:41; **4**:38; **5**:26; **8**:82; **9**:15, 17
Albright, Madeleine **9**:71
alcohol **2**:47; **4**:70; **6**:21, 22, 71

Alcott, Louisa May **4**:39
Alden, John **1**:45
Aldrin, Edwin E., Jr. **8**:36, 53, 55
Alexander, Jason **9**:95
Alexander, Lamar **9**:54
Algeria **7**:14
Ali, Muhammad (boxer) **8**:44; **9**:60
Alien and Sedition Acts **2**:49, 51
Allen, Ethan **1**:96; **2**:6
Allen, Fred **6**:35
Allen, Gracie **6**:35
Allied Powers *see* World War I; World
  War II
All in the Family **8**:65
almanacs **2**:42
alternating current **4**:51
American Broadcasting Companies
  (ABC) **9**:45
American Expeditionary Force **6**:5
American Federation of Labor (AFL)
  4:89
American Indian Movement **1**:73
"American Progress" (painting) **3**:41
American Samoa **5**:39
Americans with Disabilities Act **9**:19
American Telephone and Telegraph
  Company (AT&T) **8**:23
America Sings **9**:57
AmeriCorps **9**:75
Ames, Oates **4**:56
Amistad case **3**:28
Amos, John **8**:81
amphibious warfare **7**:14, 25, 31, 34,
  51
Amundsen, Roald **6**:42
amusement parks **6**:43, 53
amyotrophic lateral sclerosis **6**:85, 86
anarchy **5**:43; **6**:19
Anasazi **1**:7, 8, 9, 23
Anderson, Marian **6**:85
Anderson, William R. **7**:94
Andersonville Prison **4**:19
Andrea Doria, sinking of the **7**:91
Andrew (hurricane) **9**:23, 25
anesthetics **3**:31
Angelou, Maya **9**:50
animals
  buffalo, decline of **4**:42
  cloning **9**:73
  dogs as pack animals **1**:11
  Exxon Valdez oil spill's effect on
    wildlife **9**:15, 17
  horses **1**:11; **2**:41
  Miss America Pageant **6**:26
  see also birds
Annan, Kofi **9**:90
Annapolis (Maryland) **3**:39
Antarctica **3**:25; **6**:42
Anthony, Susan B. **6**:24
Antietam, Battle of **3**:86, 92, 93
Antietam National Battlefield **3**:93
anti-federalists **2**:35
antitrust laws **5**:71
Anzio, invasion at **7**:35, 36
Apaches **4**:87
Apollo program **8**:47
  Apollo 1 tragedy **8**:45
  Apollo-Soyuz Test Project **8**:76
  fire **8**:44
  Lunar Roving Vehicle **8**:64
  moon landings **8**:19, 45, 53, 55
Apollo-Soyuz Test Project **8**:76

Apple Computer Company **8**:83
Appomattox (Virginia) **4**:27, 29
Appomattox Court House National
  Historical Park **4**:29
Aquitania (ship) **5**:93
Arab-Israeli wars **8**:85
Arawak Indians **5**:37
archaeology
  1801 **2**:55
  Chaco Culture National Historical
    Park **1**:7
  Great Serpent Mound **1**:6
  Jamestown Festival Park **1**:39
  Mesa Verde National Park **1**:9
  Plimoth Plantation **1**:46
  Watson Brake Mounds **1**:5
  Wupatki National Monument **1**:8
architecture
  Empire State Building **6**:58
  Monticello **1**:83
  Shakers **3**:46
  Touro Synagogue **1**:78
  White, Stanford **5**:57
  White House **2**:53
  World's Columbian Exposition
    (1893) **5**:10
Arctic **5**:65, 66; **7**:94
Aristide, Jean-Bertrand **9**:35
Arithmetic Vulgar and Decimal **1**:68
Arizona
  1912 **5**:74
  Gadsden Purchase **3**:64
  Geronimo **4**:87
  Hoover Dam **6**:59
  Hopi Indians **1**:13
  Pueblo Indians **1**:23
  Wupatki National Monument **1**:8
Arizona, U.S.S. (ship) **7**:11
Arkansas **2**:80; **6**:45; **7**:92, 93; **9**:28, 94
Arkansas River **6**:53
Armada, Spanish **1**:32
armed forces *see* military
armored ships **3**:87
Armory Show **5**:83
arms control **8**:66
arms sales **9**:12
Armstrong, Edwin H. **6**:62
Armstrong, Louis **6**:29
Armstrong, Neil **8**:36, 53, 55, 76
Army, U.S.
  Army-McCarthy hearings **7**:86
  Army-Navy football game **3**:39
  Bosnia **9**:51
  Boxer Rebellion **5**:41
  Colt's revolver **3**:20
  Custer's Last Stand **4**:63
  early computers **7**:59
  442nd Regimental Combat Team
    7:27
  Haiti, troops in **9**:35
  integration **7**:67; **9**:87
  Jeeps **7**:28
  Pershing chases Pancho Villa
    5:90
  Rough Riders **5**:33
  Saudi Arabia, troops in **9**:19
  Trail of Tears **3**:24
  Walter Reed Medical Center **5**:34
  Westmoreland, William **8**:48
  West Point **2**:58
  Women's Army Corps **7**:22

Army, U.S. (cont.)
see also names of wars and
battles
Army Air Corps 7:22
Army Air Forces, U.S. 7:23
Army Air Service, U.S. 6:17
Army-McCarthy hearings 7:86
Arnaz, Desi 7:79
Arno, Peter 6:65
Arnold, Benedict 1:94; 2:18
Arnold, Samuel 4:33
art
Armory Show 5:83
art deco 6:49
Frick Collection 5:6
Harlem Renaissance 6:36
pop art 8:26
Taos 1:41
WPA 6:78
see also painting; photography;
sculpture
art deco 6:49
Arthur, Chester Alan 4:71, 73
Articles of Confederation 1:93; 2:9,
19, 25, 32
Ashcan School 5:80
Asian-Americans 7:5, 20
"Ask not what your country can do
for you..." 8:16
assassinations
Evers, Medgar 8:30
Garfield, James A. 4:71, 72
Kennedy, John F. 8:16, 28, 35
Kennedy, Robert F. 8:47, 52
King, Martin Luther, Jr. 8:47, 50
Lincoln, Abraham 3:81; 4:27,
30, 31, 33
Lincoln, Abraham, possible
1861 plot against 3:82
McKinley, William 5:23, 43
Reagan, Ronald, attempt on
8:91, 93
Roosevelt, Theodore, attempt
on 5:76
Astor, John Jacob 2:68
Astor, William 6:58
Astoria, Fort 2:68
astronauts see space exploration
and travel
astronomy 9:20, 32, 62, 74
Atkinson, Henry 3:12
Atlanta (Georgia) 3:48; 4:18, 24, 26;
6:52; 9:60
Atlantic Charter 6:92
Atlantic City (New Jersey) 6:26
Atlantis (space shuttle) 9:44
atomic bombs 7:54
fallout shelters 8:11
Fermi's chain reaction 7:15
Lawrence, Ernest O. 6:54
Manhattan Project 7:52
planes took off from Marianas
7:63
Rosenberg, Julius and Ethel
7:85
Strategic Air Command 7:58
Truman, Harry S. 7:45, 53
atomic energy see nuclear power
Attlee, Clement 7:53
Attucks, Crispus 1:84
Atzerodt, George 4:33
Audubon, John James 2:30; 5:88
Augusta, USS (ship) 6:92
automobiles
1908 5:60
auto racing 5:62; 9:83
Cadillac coat of arms 1:60
Capone's limousine 6:56
Ford, Henry 5:9
Ford Thunderbird 7:88
Jeeps 7:28
Model T Ford 5:61
oil embargo (1973) 8:72
Stanley Steamer 5:24
steel industry 5:40
Autry, Gene 5:79
aviation
aircraft carriers 7:13
Air Force, U.S. 7:61

airmail, early days of 5:72; 6:5
B-2 stealth bomber 9:33
B-17 "Flying Fortress" 7:23
barnstormers 6:17
Berlin airlift 7:65
Byrd, Richard E. 6:42
Coral Sea, Battle of the 7:11
Curtiss, Glenn 5:73
Doolittle's raid on Tokyo 7:7
Earhart, Amelia 6:79, 80
explosion of TWA flight 800
9:53, 59
fighter aircraft from NATO
nations 7:71
Goddard, Robert 6:41
Hindenburg disaster 6:82
jetliners 8:8
Lafayette Escadrille 5:91
Langley, Samuel 5:25
Lindbergh, Charles 6:44, 46
Midway, Battle of 7:12
Navy, United States 2:46
O'Grady, Scott 9:43
Pan Am's flying Clippers 6:77
Rodgers, Calbraith 5:71
St. Mihiel, Battle of 6:13
sound barrier, breaking of 9:83
Tuskegee airmen 7:9
U-2 incident 8:12
Wake Island airfield 6:91
women's units in World War II
7:22
Wright, Orville and Wilbur 5:49
see also space exploration and
travel

B

B-2 stealth bomber 9:33
B-17 "Flying Fortress" 7:23
Babbage, Charles 7:59
"Backyard Greenwich Village"
(painting) 5:80
Bacon, Nathaniel 1:56
Bacon's Rebellion 1:55, 56
Baekeland, Leo Hendrik 4:43
Bahamas 1:15, 16
Bailey, F. Lee 8:75
Bakelite 4:43
Baker, Ellen 9:44
Baker, Vernon 9:70
bald eagles 2:30
Ball, Lucille 7:79
balloons and ballooning 3:88
Ball's Bluff, Battle of 3:80
Baltimore (Maryland) 1:68; 2:71; 3:9;
9:49
Bancroft, George 3:39
Bank of the United States 3:6, 8
bank robberies
Bonnie and Clyde 6:66
Dillinger, John 6:70
Hearst kidnapping 8:75
Villa, Pancho 5:90
banks and banking 3:8; 5:9, 81;
6:50, 55, 67
Banneker, Benjamin 2:42
Baptists 1:67
Barbary Wars 2:46, 57
barbed wire 4:58
Barbie dolls 7:88
Bardeen, John 7:69
Barkley, Charles 9:26
barnstormers 6:17
Barnum, P.T. 4:54
Barrow, Clyde 6:66
Barry, Jack 8:6
Bartholdi, Frédéric-Auguste 4:88
Barton, Clara 4:75
baseball
1871 4:54
1941 6:90
1958 7:95
"Black Sox" scandal 6:18, 21
Coolidge throws out first pitch of
1925 season 6:33
early days of 3:42
first All-Star Game 6:67
first game under electric lights
4:79

first National League game 4:62
Gehrig, Lou 6:85, 86
Maris, Roger 8:20
Robinson, Jackie 7:60
Ruth, Babe 6:44
strike (1994) 9:34
Thomson, Bobby 7:80
Young, Cy, and first "perfect
game" 5:51
basketball 3:60; 5:5; 8:22; 9:26
Bataan 7:5, 6
Battle Above the Clouds 4:15
Bay of Pigs invasion 8:18
Beach Boys 7:88
Bean, Alan L. 8:53
beards
Gillette's razor 5:20
sideburns 3:95
Beatles, the 8:33, 90
Beatty, Warren 6:66
Beauregard, Pierre G.T. 3:85, 91
beauty contests 6:26
bebop 6:29
Becknell, William 2:83
Beckwith, Byron De La 8:30
Beecher, Henry Ward 3:68
BeeGees 8:79
Begin, Menachem 8:85
Begosh, Martin 9:51
Belgium 7:42
Bell, Alexander Graham 4:64, 65, 68
Bellamy, Francis 5:7
Belleau Wood, Battle of 6:10
Bellows, George 5:80
Bell Telephone Laboratories 7:69
Bell X-1 aircraft 9:83
belly dancing 5:10
Bennett, Floyd 6:42
Bennington, Battle of 2:16
Benny, Jack 6:35
Benoit, Joan 9:8
Benton, Thomas Hart 3:32
"Be Prepared" 5:68
Bergman, Ingrid 7:19
Berkeley, William 1:56
Berle, Milton 7:70
Berlin (Germany) 7:65; 8:29
Berlin, Irving 5:59
Berliner, Emile 4:68
Berlin airlift 7:45, 65
Berlin Wall 8:29
Bernstein, Carl 8:69
Bernstorff, Johann von 5:95
Bert the Turtle 8:11
Bessemer, Henry 5:40
Best, Pete 8:33
beverages see alcohol; Coca-Cola;
tea
B.F. Goodrich Company 5:14
Bicentennial (U.S.) 8:77
bicycles 5:19
Bienville, Jean Baptiste Le Moyne,
Sieur de 1:66
Bierstadt, Albert 2:94
big bands 6:76
"big stick" policy of Theodore
Roosevelt 5:51
Bikini Atoll 7:34
Bill of Rights 2:41
Billy the Kid 4:74
Bird, Larry 9:26
birds 1:82; 2:30; 5:88
Birdseye, Clarence 6:27
Birth of a Nation 4:41
Bismarck Sea, Battle of the 7:21
bison see buffalo
Bissell, George 3:75
Blackbeard 1:66
Black Hawk War 3:12, 56
black holes 9:62
black market 7:16
blackouts, electrical 8:41
"Black Sox" scandal 6:18, 21
"Black Tuesday" 6:55
Blackwell, Elizabeth 3:55
Blaine, James G. 4:72
Blair, James 1:63
"Bleeding Kansas" 3:63, 68
blind, braille books for 2:54

blizzards 9:67
boats and boating
flatboats 2:59
Fulton's steamboat 2:65
General Slocum disaster 5:52
Mississippi steamboats 2:93
see also ships and shipping
Boeing 707 8:8
Boeing Company 7:23; 8:64
Bogart, Humphrey 7:19
Bojaxhiu, Agnes see Teresa, Mother
Bolsheviks 6:11
bombs and bombings
attack on U.S. Marines in
Lebanon 9:5
B-2 stealth bomber 9:33
B-17 "Flying Fortress" 7:23
Bushnell's submarine Turtle
2:12
Doolittle's raid on Tokyo 7:7
Haymarket Riot 4:85, 86
Oklahoma City bombing 9:37,
42, 68, 76
Olympic Games (1996) 9:53, 60
Saudi Arabian bombing of U.S.
troops 9:58
Unabomber arrest 9:56
World Trade Center 9:29
see also atomic bombs;
hydrogen bombs
bonds, Liberty 6:6
Bonney, William H. see Billy the Kid
Bonnie and Clyde 6:66
Bonnie and Clyde (movie) 6:66
Bonus Army 6:51, 61
books see literature; publishing
Boone, Daniel 1:88
Booth, Evangeline 4:70
Booth, John Wilkes 3:81; 4:27, 30,
31, 33
bootleggers 6:21, 22
Bopp, Thomas 9:74
Borden, Amanda 9:61
Borden, Gail 3:69
Borden, Lizzie 5:13
"border ruffians" 3:68
Borglum, Gutzon 6:93
Bosnia 9:43, 51
Boston (Massachusetts)
1630 1:49
1729 1:68
Bicentennial (U.S.) 8:77
Boston Massacre 1:84
Boston Strangler 8:27
Boston Tea Party 1:85, 86
cannon of Ticonderoga 2:6
department stores 4:44
draft riots 4:13
Great Molasses Disaster 6:20
"Old Ironsides" 2:50
public libraries 4:52
subways 5:17
Boston Bruins 5:48
Boston Massacre 1:84
Boston Port Act 1:85
Boston Red Sox 7:60
Boston Strangler 8:27
Boston Tea Party 1:85, 86, 87
Bougainville 7:29
Bowie, Jim 3:17
Boxer Rebellion 5:41
boxing 4:76; 6:44; 8:44
Boyce, William D. 5:68
boycotts
Montgomery buses 7:89, 90
Olympic Games (1980) 8:88
Boy Scouts 5:68, 74; 6:6
Boys from Brazil, The 9:73
Braddock, Edward 1:74
Bradford, William 1:45
Bradley, Ed 8:51
Bradley, Omar 7:39
Brady, James 8:93
Brady, Mathew 3:81
Bragg, Braxton 3:94, 96; 4:14, 15
brakes, air 4:51
Branca, Ralph 7:80
Branch Davidians 9:30
Brattain, Walter 7:69

breakfast cereals **5**:42
Breckinridge, John C. **3**:78
Breedlove, Craig **9**:83
Breed's Hill **1**:92
bribery *see* ethics and corruption
Brice, Fanny **5**:59
bridge (card game) **6**:63
bridges
    Allies cross the Rhine **7**:48
    Brooklyn Bridge **4**:79, 80
    Golden Gate Bridge **6**:81
    Royal Gorge Bridge **6**:53
    Verrazano-Narrows Bridge **1**:20
Bridge Too Far, A (book and movie) **7**:40
Brooke, Rupert **5**:39
Brook Farm (Massachusetts) **2**:92
Brooklyn (New York) **6**:43
Brooklyn Bridge **4**:79, 80
Brooklyn Dodgers **7**:60, 80, 95
Brooks, Herb **8**:89
Brooks, James **4**:56
Brown, John **3**:68, 73, 74
brown dwarfs **9**:62
Brown University **1**:67
Brown v. *Board of Education of Topeka, Kansas* **5**:64; **7**:87
Bryan, William Jennings **6**:40
Buchanan, Daisy **6**:39
Buchanan, James **3**:71
Buchanan, Pat **9**:54
Bucher, Lloyd **8**:49
Buell, Don Carlos **3**:94
Buena Vista, Battle of **3**:49, 56
buffalo **1**:11; **4**:42
Bulge, Battle of the **7**:33, 42
Bull Moose Party *see* Progressive Party
Bull Run, First Battle of **3**:80, 85, 91
Bull Run, Second Battle of **3**:85, 90, 91
Bunker, Archie **8**:65
Bunker Hill, Battle of **1**:88, 92
Burgesses, House of **1**:37, 42
Burgoyne, John **2**:18
Burns, Anthony **3**:59
Burns, George **6**:35
Burnside, Ambrose E. **3**:95
Burr, Aaron **2**:55, 63
Burroughs, William **5**:11
Burroughs adding machine **5**:11
Burton, LeVar **8**:81
bus boycott (Montgomery, Alabama) **7**:89
Bush, George **9**:16, 19, 23
    Exxon Valdez oil spill **9**:15
    Johnson, Henry **6**:7
    Panama, U.S. invasion of **9**:18
    Presidents' Summit for America's Future **9**:75
    Yale University **1**:65
Bushnell, David **2**:12
Bwana Devil **7**:82
Byrd, Richard E. **6**:42

C

Cabeza de Vaca, Alvar Núñez **1**:21
Cabot, John **1**:17
Cabrillo, Juan Rodríguez **1**:28
Cadillac, Antoine de la Mothe **1**:60
Cajuns **1**:74
Calhoun, John C. **3**:7
California
    1846 **3**:43
    1848 **3**:53
    1850 **3**:57
    Cabrillo, Juan Rodríguez **1**:28
    covered wagons **3**:34
    Donner party **3**:47
    Drake, Sir Francis **1**:32
    El Niño storms (1998) **9**:93
    floods (1995) **9**:37, 39
    floods (1997) **9**:67
    gold rush **3**:51, 53, 54, 55
    Manifest Destiny **3**:41
    Manson murders **8**:56
    Mexico City, capture of **3**:50
    missions **1**:82
    Smith, Jedediah **2**:87

see also Los Angeles; San Francisco
California, University of **9**:32
California Institute of Technology **9**:32
Cambodia, invasion of **8**:60
Cambridge (Massachusetts) **1**:53
cameras **4**:91; **7**:64
Cameron, James **9**:86
Camp, Walter **4**:47
campaign-finance controversy **9**:77
Campanella, Roy **7**:60
Camp David Accords **8**:80, 85
Canada
    1846 **3**:43
    Cabot, John **1**:17
    Cartier, Jacques **1**:24
    Champlain, Samuel de **1**:36
    Eriksson, Leif **1**:12
    French and Indian War **1**:72
    ice hockey **5**:48
    Klondike gold rush **5**:26
    Quebec City, invasion of **1**:94
    St. Lawrence Seaway **8**:5
    Thames, Battle of the **2**:73
    War of 1812 **2**:71
    women's ice hockey **9**:88
canals
    Erie Canal **2**:91
    Nicaraguan treaty **5**:67
    Panama Canal **5**:86
    St. Lawrence Seaway **8**:5
Candler, Asa Griggs **4**:90
cannibalism of Donner party **3**:47
Cannon of Ticonderoga **2**:6
Cantigny, Battle of **6**:8
Cape Cod (Massachusetts) **1**:35, 38, 44
Capital Cities/ABC **9**:45
capital punishment
    Andersonville Prison's commander **4**:19
    colonial punishments **1**:57
    electricity **4**:51
    Guiteau, Charles Julius **4**:72
    Hale, Nathan **2**:11
    Lindbergh kidnapping **6**:64
    Rosenberg, Julius and Ethel **7**:85
    Sacco-Vanzetti case **6**:23
    Salem witch-hunt **1**:62
    Turner, Nat **3**:11
    Vesey, Denmark **2**:84
Capitol, U.S. **2**:45, 52, 74
Capone, Al **6**:44, 56, 71
card games **6**:63
Caribbean Sea and islands **1**:15, 64; **5**:28; **9**:6
Carlson, Chester **6**:84
Carnegie, Andrew **4**:52; **5**:6, 40
Carpenter's Hall **2**:9
Carraway, Nick **6**:39
Carrier, Willis **5**:47
Carson, Kit **1**:41
Carter, Edward **9**:70
Carter, Jimmy **8**:77, 80, 88
    Camp David Accords **8**:85
    Ford, Gerald R. **8**:74
    Hearst, Patty **8**:75
    Iranian hostage crisis **8**:87, 91
    Presidents' Summit for America's Future **9**:75
Cartier, Jacques **1**:24
cartoons, editorial
    Alaska, purchase of **4**:38
    Credit Mobilier scandal **4**:56
    Eaton, Peggy **3**:7
    Hawaii, annexation of **5**:35
    income tax **5**:82
    Jackson versus the Bank of the United States **3**:8
    Johnson, Andrew, impeachment trial **4**:39
    New Deal **6**:67
    Panic of 1893 **5**:9
    Paxton Boys **1**:77
    Red Scare of 1919–1920 **6**:19
    Roosevelt, Theodore, and "big stick" policy **5**:51

Roosevelt, Theodore, ending Russo-Japanese War **5**:53
    Sherman Antitrust Act **4**:95
    Social Security Act **6**:75
    Teapot Dome scandal **6**:34
    Uncle Sam **2**:77
    Zimmermann Telegram **5**:95
Cartwright, Alexander **3**:42
Caruso, Enrico **5**:69
Casablanca (movie) **7**:19
cash registers **4**:69
casinos *see* gambling
Cassini space probe **9**:84
Castillo, Alonso del **1**:21
Castro, Fidel **8**:18
Cather, Willa **1**:41
Catlin, George **2**:79
Catt, Carrie Chapman **6**:21
cattle drives **4**:37
Catton, Bruce **3**:96
Caverly, John R. **6**:38
CD-ROMs **8**:83; **9**:7
CDs *see* compact discs
Cedar Creek, Battle of **4**:25
celluloid **4**:43
census, U.S. **7**:59
Centennial Exposition **4**:62, 64
Central Intelligence Agency (CIA) **8**:12, 18; **9**:16
Central Pacific Railroad **4**:46
Central Park (New York City) **8**:90
cereals *see* breakfast cereals
Cézanne, Paul **5**:83
Chaco Culture National Historical Park **1**:7
Chafee, John **8**:49
Chaffee, Roger **8**:39, 45
chain reaction **7**:15
chain stores **4**:44
Challenger disaster **9**:11
Chamberlain, Wilt **8**:22
Chamorros **5**:36; **7**:63
Champlain, Lake **1**:36
Champlain, Samuel de **1**:36, 52
Chancellorsville, Battle of **4**:8
Chaney, James **8**:34
Chaplin, Charlie **5**:50
Chapman, Mark David **8**:90
Chapultepec **3**:50
Charlesfort (South Carolina settlement) **1**:29
Charleston (South Carolina) **3**:84; **4**:12
Charlestown (Massachusetts) **1**:88, 92
Château-Thierry, Battle of **6**:9
Chattanooga, Battle of **4**:15
Cherokee Nation **1**:10; **2**:75; **3**:24; **4**:14
Chesapeake (ship) **2**:46
chess **8**:66
chewing gum **5**:85
Cheyenne Indians **4**:63
Chicago (Illinois)
    bicycles **5**:19
    Capone, Al **6**:56
    department stores **4**:44
    fire (1871) **4**:54
    Haymarket Riot **4**:85, 86
    Pullman's factory town **4**:36
    St. Valentine's Day Massacre **6**:56
    World's Columbian Exposition (1893) **5**:10
Chicago White Sox **6**:18, 21
Chickamauga, Battle of **4**:14
child labor **4**:57, 95; **5**:81
children
    Boy Scouts **5**:68
    breakfast cereals **5**:42
    child labor **4**:57
    Dare, Virginia, first British child born in North America **1**:34
    Earth Day **8**:61
    Girl Scouts **5**:77
    McCaughey septuplets **9**:85
    public education **5**:12
    Sesame Street **8**:58

"Stand for Children" **9**:57
    see also toys and games
Children's Defense Fund **9**:57
Children's Television Workshop **8**:58
Chilkoot Trail **5**:26
China **2**:43; **5**:41; **8**:54, 66; **9**:47
China Clipper (airplane) **6**:77, 91
Chinese in America **4**:46, 79, 85
Chippewa *see* Ojibwe
Chiricahua Apaches **4**:87
Choltitz, Dietrich von **7**:39
Chow, Amy **9**:61
Christ Church (Philadelphia) **2**:9
Christianity
    arson of African-American churches **9**:52
    California missions **1**:82
    Great Awakening **1**:67
    Promise Keepers rally **9**:82
    Puritans **1**:49, 53
    Salvation Army **4**:70
    Scopes trial **6**:40
    Shakers **3**:46
    YMCA **3**:60
    see also Roman Catholics in America
Christopher, Warren **9**:71
Chrysler Building **6**:49
Chrysler Corporation **7**:28
Church, Frederick **2**:94
church arson **9**:52
Churchill, Winston **6**:92; **7**:46, 53
Church of Jesus Christ of Latter-day Saints *see* Mormons
CIA **8**:12, 18; **9**:16
Cíbola, Seven Cities of **1**:21, 22, 25, 26
Cincinnati (Ohio) **6**:49
Cinque **3**:28
circus **4**:54
Citizen Kane **6**:95
citizenship **2**:51; **3**:83; **4**:39; **5**:37
civil disobedience **3**:43
civil rights
    Bill of Rights **2**:41
    Miranda decision **8**:42
    Scottsboro case **6**:60
Civil Rights Act of 1964 **8**:9, 31
civil-rights movement
    1963 **8**:28
    desegregation of the armed forces **7**:67; **9**:87
    Evers, Medgar **8**:30
    Freedom Summer murders **8**:34
    Johnson, Lyndon Baines **8**:32
    King, Martin Luther, Jr. **8**:50
    Ku Klux Klan **4**:41
    Little Rock school integration **7**:92, 93
    march on Washington **8**:31
    Martin Luther King, Jr., National Historic Site **6**:52
    Meredith, James **8**:24
    Montgomery bus boycott **7**:89
    NAACP **5**:64
    Selma-to-Montgomery marches **8**:37
    sit-ins **8**:9
civil service **4**:67, 73; **7**:67
Civil War, U.S. **3**:80, 86; **4**:5, 18, 27
    Andersonville Prison **4**:19
    Antietam, Battle of **3**:92, 93
    Appomattox Court House **4**:29
    baseball, early days of **3**:42
    Borden's condensed milk **3**:69
    Bull Run, First Battle of **3**:85
    Bull Run, Second Battle of **3**:90
    Chancellorsville, Battle of **4**:8
    Chattanooga, Battle of **4**:15
    Chickamauga, Battle of **4**:14
    Colt's revolver **3**:20
    Davis, Jefferson **3**:83
    draft riots (1863) **4**:13
    Emancipation Proclamation **4**:6
    events leading to **3**:78
    Fort Sumter National Monument **3**:84
    Fort Wagner, Battle of **4**:12
    Fredericksburg, Battle of **3**:95

Civil War, U.S. (cont.)
Frémont, John C. **3**:32
Garfield, James A. **4**:71
Gettysburg, Battle of **4**:10, 11
Gettysburg Address **4**:16
Gone With the Wind **6**:87
Grant, Ulysses S. **4**:45
Grant's capture of Richmond **4**:28
Harrison, Benjamin **4**:92
Hayes, Rutherford B. **4**:67
income tax **5**:82
Johnson, Andrew **4**:32
Kearsarge vs. *Alabama* **4**:23
Kennesaw Mountain, Battle of **4**:24
Lincoln, Abraham **3**:81
Manassas National Battlefield Park **3**:91
Medal of Honor **4**:7
Monitor vs. the *Merrimack* **3**:87
Mosby's Rangers **4**:17
Murfreesboro, Battle of **3**:96
Peninsular Campaign **3**:88
Perryville, Battle of **3**:94
Petersburg, Siege of **4**:22
Sherman's March to the Sea **4**:26
Shiloh, Battle of **3**:89
Sons of Liberty **1**:79
South Carolina, secession of **3**:79
Spotsylvania, Battle of **4**:21
uniforms made by sewing machine **3**:44
Vicksburg, Siege of **4**:9
Wilderness, Battle of the **4**:20
Wilkes, Charles **3**:25
Clark, Mark **7**:26
Clark, William **2**:62
classified information **8**:63
Clay, Henry **2**:89, 90; **3**:57, 62
Clermont (boat) **2**:65
Cleveland, Frances Folsom **4**:84
Cleveland, Grover **4**:84, 85; **5**:35
Cliff Palace **1**:9
Clinton, Bill **9**:23, 28, 34, 53, 68
Africa, visit to **9**:92
Albright, Madeleine **9**:71
campaign-finance controversy **9**:77
church arson sites, visit to **9**:52
election (1996) **9**:66
50th anniversary of end of World War II **9**:48
Iraq crisis (1997–1998) **9**:90
John Paul II's 1995 visit to U.S. **9**:49
Medal of Honor given to African-American veterans by **9**:70
Presidents' Summit for America's Future **9**:75
Republican control of Congress **9**:38
Saudi Arabian bombing of U.S. troops **9**:58
scandals **9**:96
second inauguration **9**:69
U.S. conflict with Iraq **9**:64
welfare reform **9**:63
Yale University **1**:65
Clinton, Chelsea **9**:53, 69
Clinton, DeWitt **2**:91
Clinton, Henry **2**:23
Clinton, Hillary Rodham **1**:65; **9**:47, 53, 69, 96
clipper ships **3**:51
cloning **9**:68, 73
Clooney, George **9**:36
clothing and fashion
1619 **1**:42
flappers **6**:30
Godey's Lady's Book **3**:10
Samoan wraparound cloth **5**:39
zippers **5**:14
coal **5**:40
Coast Guard, U.S. **2**:40; **7**:22
Coast Guard Academy, U.S. **2**:40
Cobb, Lee J. **7**:72

Coca-Cola **4**:90
Cochran, Johnnie **9**:40
Code Talkers **7**:10
coeducation **3**:13
Coercive Acts *see* Intolerable Acts
Coffin, Levi **3**:21
cog railways **4**:49
Cohoninas **1**:8
Cold War **7**:73, 95
Army-McCarthy hearings **7**:86
fallout shelters **8**:11
NATO **7**:71
Potsdam Conference **7**:53
Rosenberg, Julius and Ethel **7**:85
Cole, Thomas **2**:94
Colfax, Schuyler **4**:56
colleges and universities
Coast Guard Academy **2**:40
desegregation **8**:21, 24
first U.S. medical school **1**:81
football, early days of **4**:47
G.I. Bill **7**:43
Great Awakening **1**:67
Harvard College founding **1**:53
Kent State killings **8**:62
Naval Academy **3**:39
Oberlin College **3**:13
student protests **8**:59
West Point **2**:58
William and Mary, College of **1**:63
Yale University **1**:65
Collins, Michael **8**:36, 55
colonial life in America
Great Awakening **1**:67
punishments **1**:57
stagecoaches **2**:85
Yankee peddlers **2**:44
Colorado **1**:9; **2**:64; **3**:73; **5**:87; **6**:53
Colorado River **4**:53; **6**:59; **9**:55
color television **7**:76
Colt, Samuel **3**:20
Colter, John **4**:55
Columbia (space shuttle) **8**:91, 94
Columbia, District of *see* Washington (D.C.)
Columbia Broadcasting System (CBS) **7**:76; **8**:51; **9**:45
Columbia River **2**:43, 68; **6**:94
Columbus, Christopher **1**:15, 16; **5**:10, 37; **9**:23
Comanches **2**:87
Comet (airplane) **8**:8
comet Hale-Bopp **9**:68, 74
comic strips **5**:18
Comiskey, Charles **6**:18
communications
Bell, Alexander Graham **4**:64
Code Talkers **7**:10
De Forest, Lee **5**:69
early telephones **4**:65
telegraph **3**:37
Telstar I **8**:23
Communism
1950 **7**:73
Army-McCarthy hearings **7**:86
Bay of Pigs invasion **8**:18
Grenada, invasion of **9**:6
NATO guarded against **7**:71
Red Scare of 1919–1920 **6**:19
community service **9**:75
Como, Perry **6**:76
compact discs (CDs) **9**:7
Compromise of 1850 **3**:57, 58, 59
Compulsion **6**:38
computers **7**:59, 69, 76; **8**:83; **9**:7
Comstock Lode **3**:73, 76
condensed milk **3**:69
Conestoga Indians **1**:77
Coney Island **6**:43
Confederate States of America
1861 **3**:83
Andersonville Prison **4**:19
Davis, Jefferson **3**:83
Mosby's Rangers **4**:17

South Carolina, secession of **3**:79
Congregationalists **1**:67
Congress, Library of *see* Library of Congress
Congress, U.S.
1787 **2**:32
1789 **2**:37
Credit Mobilier scandal **4**:56
Iran-contra affair **9**:12
Republican control **9**:37, 38, 66
Secret Service **4**:72
slave trade, end of the **2**:65
Women's Army Corps **7**:22
see also House of Representatives, U.S.; Senate, U.S.
Congress Hall **2**:9
Congress of Confederation **1**:93
Connecticut **1**:65, 90; **2**:40; **3**:20, 28
Connolly, James **5**:21
conquistadors **1**:30
Conrad, Charles, Jr. **8**:53
conscientious objectors **4**:13
conservation *see* environment
Constitution, USS (ship) *see* "Old Ironsides"
Constitutional Convention **2**:33, 38, 49
Constitution of the U.S. **2**:32
Articles of Confederation **2**:19
Bill of Rights **2**:41
citizenship to former slaves **4**:39
Constitutional Convention **2**:33
Federalist Papers, The **2**:34
income tax **5**:82
Independence National Historical Park **2**:9
Madison, James **2**:67
Marbury v. Madison **2**:61
presidential elections **2**:55
presidential term limitation **6**:68, 88; **7**:76
Prohibition **6**:22, 71
ratification **2**:35
slavery abolished **4**:27
200th anniversary of signing **9**:13
woman suffrage **6**:24
Continental Congress, First **1**:87
Continental Congress, Second **1**:93, 95; **2**:5, 7
Contract with America **9**:34, 38
contras **9**:12, 13
Cook, James **2**:22; **5**:35
Coolidge, Calvin **6**:32, 33, 44
Cooney, Joan Ganz **8**:58
Cooper, Ann Julia **3**:13
Cooper, Gary **6**:14
Cooper, L. Gordon **8**:28
Cooper, Peter **3**:9
cooperatives **4**:61
Copperheads **4**:18
Coppola, "Trigger Mike" **7**:78
Coral Sea, Battle of the **7**:11, 13
Corbett, James J. **4**:76
Cornwallis, Lord **2**:17, 25, 27, 28
Coronado, Francisco Vásquez de **1**:22, 25, 26
Corregidor **7**:6
corruption *see* ethics and corruption
Cosby, Bill **9**:10
Cosby Show, The **9**:10
cotton **2**:39, 60
cotton gin **2**:45, 48
Coubertin, Pierre de **5**:21
covered wagons **2**:83; **3**:33, 34
cowboys **4**:37
Cowpens, Battle of **2**:26
Coxey, Jacob **5**:15
"Coxey's Army" **5**:15
crafts, Shaker **3**:46
Craig, Jim **8**:89
Crazy Horse **4**:63
Credit Mobilier scandal **4**:56
Creek Indians **2**:75, 89
Crichton, Michael **9**:36

crime
Bonnie and Clyde **6**:66
Capone, Al **6**:56
Dillinger, John **6**:70
Kefauver Crime Commission **7**:78
Miranda decision **8**:42
see also murder
Crippen, Robert **8**:94
Crisis (magazine) **5**:64
Crockett, Davy **3**:17
Croix de Guerre **6**:7
Crothers, Scatman **8**:81
Crucible, The **1**:62
Cuba
1898 **5**:27
Bay of Pigs invasion **8**:18
Cuban missile crisis **8**:21, 25
Maine, USS, sinking of the **5**:29
Manifest Destiny **3**:41
McKinley, William **5**:23
Reed, Walter **5**:34
Rough Riders **5**:33
Spanish-American War **5**:28; **9**:91
Cuban missile crisis **8**:21, 25
Culbertson, Ely **6**:63
Cullen, Countee **6**:36
cults **9**:30
Currier & Ives **4**:54
Curtiss, Glenn **5**:73
Custer, George **4**:63
Custer's Last Stand **4**:62, 63
cyclotron **6**:54
Czolgosz, Leon **5**:23, 43

D

Dakota Indians *see* Sioux Indians
Daley, Chuck **9**:26
dams **4**:93; **6**:59, 72, 94
DaNang (Vietnam) **8**:38
dance
dance marathons **6**:37
disco dancing **8**:79
flappers **6**:30
Hopi snake dance **1**:6, 13
jazz **6**:29
see also musical theater
Dandridge, Dorothy **6**:74
Dare, Virginia **1**:33, 34
Darrow, Clarence **6**:38, 40
Dartmouth College **1**:67
Daughters of the American Revolution **6**:85
Dauphine (ship) **1**:20
Davies, Samuel **1**:67
Davis, Benjamin O. **9**:87
Davis, Benjamin O., Jr. **7**:9; **9**:87
Davis, Jefferson **3**:56, 83, 94
Davis, Miles **6**:29
Dawes, Dominique **9**:61
Dawes, William **1**:88
Day, Doris **6**:76
Dayton Accord **9**:51
D-Day **7**:8, 22, 33, 38, 39; **9**:34
DDT **2**:30
deafness **4**:64
Death of a Salesman **7**:72
death penalty *see* capital punishment
debates
Kennedy-Nixon debates **8**:14
Lincoln-Douglas debates **3**:72
Debs, Eugene V. **5**:16, 76
Decatur, Stephen **2**:57
Declaration of Independence **2**:7
1776 **2**:5
Adams, John **2**:49
Independence National Historical Park **2**:9
Jefferson, Thomas **2**:56
Liberty Bell **2**:8
Second Continental Congress **1**:93
Declaration of Sentiments **3**:52
Deere, John **3**:26
Deerhound (ship) **4**:23
De Forest, Lee **5**:69
Delaware **1**:48; **2**:32

de Mille, Agnes **7:**32
Democratic Party **3:**78; **8:**47; **9:**9, 77
Democratic Republican Party **2:**89
demonstrations and protests
  Bonus Army **6:**61
  Cambodia, invasion of **8:**60
  civil-rights sit-ins **8:**9
  "Coxey's Army" **5:**15
  Kent State killings **8:**62
  march on Washington **8:**31
  Selma-to-Montgomery marches
    8:37
  Shays' Rebellion **2:**31
  Vietnam War **8:**38, 44, 47, 53,
    59
  Whiskey Rebellion **2:**47
  see also rallies; riots
Dempsey, Jack **6:**44
Denver (Colorado) **9:**76
department stores **4:**44
deportation **6:**19
Depression of the 1930's **6:**50, 67,
    73
  "Black Tuesday" **6:**55
  Bonus Army **6:**61
  dance marathons **6:**37
  election of 1932 **6:**65
  Hoover, Herbert **6:**51
  Roosevelt, Franklin D. **6:**68
  welfare system **9:**63
  WPA **6:**78
depressions, economic
  1819 **2:**80
  1837 **3:**8
  Panic of 1893 **5:**9
  Van Buren, Martin **3:**22
  see also Depression of the
    1930's
DeSalvo, Albert see Boston
    Strangler
desegregation
  armed forces **7:**9, 67; **9:**87
  Brown v. Board of Education
    7:87
  Civil Rights Act of 1964 **8:**31
  Little Rock school integration
    7:92, 93
  Meredith, James **8:**21, 24
  Oberlin College admits blacks
    3:13
  public schools **5:**64
  see also segregation
"Desert Fox" see Rommel, Erwin
Desert Storm, Operation see Persian
    Gulf War
desktop publishing **8:**83
de Soto, Hernando **1:**26, 27
Detroit (Michigan) **1:**60; **8:**44
Dewey, George **5:**27, 28, 30, 31;
    9:91
Dewey, Thomas **7:**33, 66
Dezhurov, Vladimir **9:**44
Dial M for Murder **7:**82
Diana, Princess of Wales **9:**68
DiCaprio, Leonardo **9:**86
Dickinson, John **2:**19
dictionaries **2:**95
Dillinger, John **6:**70
DiMaggio, Joe **6:**90
dirigibles **6:**82
disabled people **8:**40; **9:**19
disaster relief **4:**75
disasters
  Andrea Doria sinking **7:**91
  Challenger disaster **9:**11
  explosion of TWA flight 800
    9:53, 59
  General Slocum disaster **5:**52
  Great Molasses Disaster **6:**20
  Hindenburg **6:**79, 82
  Titanic sinking **5:**75
  see also floods; hurricanes
disco dancing **8:**79
Discovery (Cook's ship) **2:**22
Discovery (Hudson's ship) **1:**40
Discovery (space shuttle) **8:**94; **9:**20
Discovery (Virginia colonists' ship)
    1:37, 39

discrimination see prejudice and
    discrimination
diseases see medicine and health
Distinguished Flying Cross **7:**9
District of Columbia see Washington
    (D.C.)
Dixie Queen (show boat) **6:**48
"Do a Good Turn Daily" **5:**68
dogs as pack animals **1:**11
Dole, Robert **8:**40, 77; **9:**38, 53, 54,
    66
Dole, Sanford B. **5:**9, 35
Dolly (cloned sheep) **9:**73
Donner party **3:**47
"Don't give up the ship!" **2:**46
Doolittle, Jimmy **7:**7
"Doonesbury" **5:**18
Dorantes, Andrés **1:**21
Dorsey, Tommy and Jimmy **6:**76
Doublemint chewing gum **5:**85
doughboys **6:**9, 12
Douglas, Stephen A. **3:**72, 78
Douglass, Frederick **3:**21, 52, 62
Douglass, Rosetta **3:**13
"doves" (opponents of Vietnam War)
    8:38
draft **6:**89
draft riots (1863) **4:**13
Drake, Edwin **3:**73, 75
Drake, Sir Francis **1:**31, 32
drama see theater
"Dream Team" **9:**26
Dred Scott decision **3:**70
Drexler, Clyde **9:**26
drought and Dust Bowl **6:**57
drug industry **3:**31; **5:**56
DuBois, W.E.B. **5:**64; **6:**36
Duchamp, Marcel **5:**83
duels **1:**38; **2:**63
due process **6:**60
Dunant, Henri **4:**75
Dunaway, Faye **6:**66
Dunbar, Bonnie **9:**44
Dunster, Henry **1:**53
Dust Bowl **6:**57
Dutch in America **1:**48
Dutch Reformed Church **1:**67

E

Eagle (British ship) **2:**12
eagles **2:**30
Eagle Scout **5:**68
Earhart, Amelia **6:**79, 80
Early, Jubal **4:**25
Earp, Wyatt **3:**20
Earth Day **8:**59, 61
earthquakes
  Los Angeles (1992) **9:**23
  Los Angeles (1994) **9:**34
  San Francisco (1906) **5:**54, 55
  San Francisco (1989) **9:**15
Eastman, George **4:**91
Eaton, John **3:**7
Eaton, Peggy **3:**7
Ebert, Roger **9:**95
Eclipse (steamboat) **2:**93
Edelman, Marian Wright **9:**57
Edison, Thomas Alva **4:**51, 68; **5:**9;
    9:72
Ed Sullivan Show, The **7:**90; **8:**33
education
  Cherokee Nation **1:**10
  desegregation **5:**64; **7:**87, 92,
    93
  G.I. Bill **7:**43
  prayer in public schools **8:**21
  public education **5:**12
  public libraries **4:**52
  Sesame Street **8:**58
  Webster's dictionary **2:**95
  WPA **6:**78
  see also colleges and
    universities
Edwards, Anthony **9:**36
Edwards, Jonathan **1:**67
Egypt **7:**90; **8:**85
Einstein, Albert **7:**85
Eisenhower, David **8:**85

Eisenhower, Dwight D. **7:**21, 33, 81,
    84, 90, 92, 95
  Allies cross the Rhine **7:**48
  D-Day **7:**38
  former general elected
    president **9:**46
  Kasserine Pass, Battle of the
    7:24
  Little Rock school integration
    7:93
  Market-Garden, Operation **7:**40
  North Africa, invasion of **7:**14
  U-2 incident **8:**12
  West Point **2:**58
Eisenhower, Mamie **7:**92
Eisner, Michael **9:**45
Elbe River **7:**50
elderly see aging and aged
elections, presidential
  1800 **2:**55
  1824 **2:**89, 90
  1860 **3:**78
  1864 **4:**18
  1876 **4:**62, 66, 67
  1908 **5:**60
  1912 **5:**63, 74, 76
  1932 **6:**65
  1948 **7:**66
  1952 **7:**81
  1968 **8:**47
  1976 **8:**77
  1980 **8:**88
  1992 **9:**23
  1996 **8:**40; **9:**66
  campaign-finance controversy
    9:77
  Kennedy-Nixon debates **8:**14
  Republican control of Congress
    (1994) **9:**38
  Republican primaries (1996)
    9:53, 54
  Roosevelt's third term **6:**88
  12th Amendment to Constitution
    2:55
electoral votes **4:**66, 67
electricity
  blackout of 1965 **8:**41
  first baseball game under
    electric lights **4:**79
  Grand Coulee Dam **6:**94
  Hoover Dam **6:**59
  Tennessee Valley Authority **6:**72
  Three Mile Island accident **8:**86
  Westinghouse, George **4:**51
  World's Columbian Exposition
    (1893) **5:**10
electronics **7:**69; **8:**83
elevators **3:**67, 73
Elizabeth (English queen; consort of
    George VI) **6:**69
Elizabeth I (queen of England) **1:**32
Elizabeth II (queen of Great Britain)
    7:92
Elk Hill (California) **6:**34
Ellington, Duke **6:**29, 76
Ellis Island **4:**88; **5:**8
Ellsberg, Daniel **8:**63
El Niño **9:**39, 93, 94
Ely, Eugene **7:**13
Emancipation Proclamation **3:**86;
    4:5, 6, 54
embargo, oil (1973) **8:**72
Emerson, John **3:**70
Emerson, Ralph Waldo **3:**59
Emmy Awards **8:**81; **9:**36
Emory University **4:**90
Empire State Building **6:**58
Empire Strikes Back, The **8:**84
endangered and extinct species
    2:30; **4:**42; **5:**88
Endeavour (space shuttle) **9:**20
Enewetok Atoll **7:**34
engineering **4:**80; **5:**86
English language **2:**95
ENIAC **7:**59
Enola Gay (airplane) **7:**54
Enterprise (aircraft carrier) **7:**13
Enterprise (space shuttle) **8:**94

entertainment see movies;
    television; theater; the
    names of sports
environment
  air conditioners **5:**47
  Earth Day **8:**59, 61
  Exxon Valdez oil spill **9:**15, 17
  Grand Canyon, artificial flood in
    9:55
  Persian Gulf War damage **9:**21
  plastics, disposal of **4:**43
  Powell, John Wesley **4:**53
  Roosevelt, Theodore **5:**45
epidemic, influenza (1918) **6:**16
E Pluribus Unum **2:**5
Equality State **4:**48
ER **9:**36
"Era of Good Feeling" **2:**78
Erie, Lake, Battle of **2:**72, 73; **3:**65
Erie Canal **2:**89, 91
Eriksson, Leif **1:**12
Erik the Red **1:**12
erosion and Dust Bowl **6:**57
Eruzione, Mike **8:**89
espionage
  Hale, Nathan **2:**11
  Pueblo incident **8:**49
  Rosenberg, Julius and Ethel
    7:85
  U-2 incident **8:**12
Estéban (Estevánico) **1:**21, 22
E.T., the Extra-Terrestrial **8:**95
ether **3:**31
ethics and corruption
  Arthur, Chester Alan **4:**73
  "Black Sox" scandal **6:**18, 21
  campaign-finance controversy
    9:77
  "Checkers" speech **7:**81
  Clinton scandals **9:**96
  cloning **9:**73
  Credit Mobilier scandal **4:**56
  Grant administration **4:**56
  Harding, Warren G. **6:**25, 32
  Kefauver Crime Commission
    7:78
  quiz show scandal **8:**6
  Teapot Dome scandal **6:**34
  Tweed, "Boss" **4:**54
  Watergate scandal **8:**54, 67
ethnic groups see African-
    Americans; Native
    Americans
Europe and Marshall Plan **7:**68
"Evangeline" **1:**74
Everett, Edward **4:**16
Everglades **2:**79
Evers, Medgar **8:**30
Evers-Williams, Myrlie **8:**30
evolution **6:**40
Ewing, Patrick **9:**26
execution see capital punishment
exploration and discovery
  1541 **1:**26
  Byrd, Richard E. **6:**42
  Cabeza de Vaca expedition
    1:21
  Cabot, John **1:**17
  Cabrillo, Juan Rodríguez **1:**28
  Cadillac, Antoine de la Mothe
    1:60
  Cartier, Jacques **1:**24
  Champlain, Samuel de **1:**36
  Columbus, Christopher **1:**15, 16
  Cook's discovery of Hawaii **2:**22
  Coronado, Francisco Vásquez
    de **1:**25
  de Soto, Hernando **1:**27
  Drake, Sir Francis **1:**32
  Earhart, Amelia **6:**80
  Eriksson, Leif **1:**12
  Estéban **1:**22
  Frémont, John C. **3:**32
  Gosnold, Bartholomew **1:**35
  Gray, Robert **2:**43
  Henson, Matthew **5:**66
  Hudson, Henry **1:**40
  La Salle, Sieur de **1:**59
  Lewis and Clark expedition **2:**62

exploration and discovery (cont.)
Long, Stephen H. **2**:81
Marquette and Jolliet **1**:54
Nautilus **7**:94
Nicolet, Jean **1**:52
Oñate, Juan de **1**:30
Peary, Robert E. **5**:65
Pike, Zebulon **2**:64
Ponce de León, Juan **1**:19
Powell, John Wesley **4**:53
Ribaut, Jean **1**:29
Smith, Jedediah **2**:87
Verrazano, Giovanni da **1**:20
Vespucci, Amerigo **1**:18
Wilkes expedition **3**:25
see also space exploration and travel
Explorer I (satellite) **7**:95
explosions
Challenger disaster **9**:11
Great Molasses Disaster **6**:20
Hindenburg disaster **6**:79, 82
Maine, USS, sinking of the **5**:28, 29
Petersburg, Siege of **4**:22
TWA flight 800 **9**:53, 59
see also atomic bombs; bombs and bombings
extinct species *see* endangered and extinct species
extraterrestrial life **8**:78; **9**:78
Exxon Valdez oil spill **9**:15, 17

F

Fairbanks, Douglas **6**:6
Fair Labor Standards Act **4**:57
fairs and expositions
Centennial Exposition (1876) **4**:64
Louisiana Purchase Exposition (1904) **5**:51
World's Columbian Exposition (1893) **5**:10
World's Fair (1939) introduces television **6**:85; **7**:70
Fall, Albert B. **6**:25, 34
fallout shelters **8**:11
Fall River (Massachusetts) **5**:13
Family, the **8**:56
famine **1**:37; **9**:27
Fargo (North Dakota) **9**:67
Farmer's Almanac, The **2**:42
Farrakhan, Louis **9**:50
fashion *see* clothing and fashion
Faubus, Orval **7**:92, 93
Federal Bureau of Investigation (FBI) **4**:41; **8**:34; **9**:30, 56
Federalist Papers, The **2**:34, 67
federalists **2**:35
Federal Reserve System **3**:8
Fenian Ram (submarine) **5**:38
Ferber, Edna **6**:48
Ferdinand (king of Spain) **1**:16
Ferguson, John H. **5**:22
Ferguson, Patrick **2**:24
Fermi, Enrico **7**:15
Ferraro, Geraldine **9**:8, 9
Ferris Wheel **5**:10
feud of Hatfields and McCoys **4**:77
Fields, W.C. **5**:59
"Fifty-four forty or fight!" **3**:43
54th Massachusetts Regiment **4**:12
"fighting leathernecks" **1**:95
Filene, Edward **4**:44
Fillmore, Millard **3**:57, 58
Finn, Huckleberry **4**:83
firearms *see* guns
fires
Apollo 1 tragedy **8**:39, 44, 45
arson of African-American churches **9**:52
Atlanta (1864) **4**:26
Chicago (1871) **4**:54
General Slocum disaster **5**:52
Grand Forks (North Dakota, 1997) **9**:67
Johnstown flood **4**:93
San Francisco earthquake (1906) **5**:54, 55

Triangle fire **5**:70, 71
Waco raid **9**:30
Washington (D.C.) (1814) **2**:74
Yellowstone National Park **9**:14
see also explosions
"fireside chats" **6**:35, 68
First Continental Congress **1**:87
'First in war, first in peace, and first in the hearts of his countrymen' **2**:38
Fischer, Bobby **8**:66
fish **9**:93
Fisher, Carrie **8**:84
Fisher's Hill, Battle of **4**:25
Fitzgerald, Ella **6**:76
Fitzgerald, F. Scott **6**:39
five-and-dime stores **9**:80
flag, American **2**:16; **5**:7; **8**:15
Flagg, James Montgomery **6**:6
flappers **6**:30
Fletcher, Frank J. **7**:11
floods
California (1995) **9**:37, 39
Grand Canyon, artificial flood in **9**:55
Great Flood of 1993 **9**:31
Johnstown (Pennsylvania) **4**:93
Mississippi River (1927) **6**:45
Tennessee River **6**:72
upper Midwest (1996–1997) **9**:67, 68
Florida
1819 **2**:80
hurricane Andrew **9**:23, 25
Ponce de León, Juan **1**:19
Ribaut, Jean **1**:29
St. Augustine **1**:31
Seminole Wars **2**:79
takeover by U.S. **2**:82
tornadoes (1998) **9**:94
fluorocarbons **5**:47
Flyer (airplane) **5**:49
"flying boats" **5**:73
FM radio **6**:62
Foch, Ferdinand **6**:12
folklore *see* legends and folklore
folk music **8**:57
Folsom, Frances **4**:85
Fontana Dam **6**:72
food
Birdseye's frozen foods **6**:27
Borden's condensed milk **3**:69
breakfast cereals **5**:42
Coca-Cola **4**:90
Louisiana Purchase Exposition (1904) **5**:51
microwave ovens **8**:46
Pure Food and Drug Act (1906) **5**:54, 56
rationing **7**:16
TV dinners **7**:70
victory gardens **7**:18
football **1**:65; **3**:39; **4**:47; **6**:67; **8**:44
Forbes, Steve **9**:54
Ford, Betty **8**:67
Ford, Gerald R. **8**:67, 73, 74, 77
Presidents' Summit for America's Future **9**:75
Warren Commission Report **8**:35
Watergate scandal **8**:67
Ford, Harrison **8**:84
Ford, Henry **5**:9, 60, 61
Ford, Thomas **3**:36
Ford Motor Company **7**:88
Ford's Theatre **4**:30, 31
foreign policy
Bay of Pigs invasion **8**:18
Marshall Plan **7**:68
Monroe, James **2**:78
Monroe Doctrine **2**:88
forest fires **9**:14
Fort Astoria **2**:68
Fort McHenry **2**:71
Fort Moultrie **3**:84
Fort Riley **6**:16
Fort Rosalie **1**:68; **3**:40
Fort Sumter **3**:79, 80, 84

Fort Sumter National Monument **3**:84
Fort Ticonderoga **1**:96; **2**:6
Fort Wagner, Battle of **4**:12
Fort Wayne (Indiana) **4**:79
forty-niners **3**:54, 55
"Forward America" **5**:68
fossils *see* archaeology
Foster, Jodie **8**:93
Fountain of Youth **1**:19
Fourteen Points **6**:5, 15
Fourth of July, presidents' deaths on **2**:78
Fox, John **9**:70
France
Belleau Wood, Battle of **6**:10
Cantigny, Battle of **6**:8
Cartier, Jacques **1**:24
Château-Thierry, Battle of **6**:9
D-Day **7**:38
French and Indian War **1**:72
Johnson, Henry **6**:7
Lafayette Escadrille **5**:91
Marne, Second Battle of the **6**:12
Meuse-Argonne offensive **6**:14
Paris, liberation of **7**:39
Paris, Treaty of **2**:29
St. Mihiel, Battle of **6**:13
Statue of Liberty **4**:88
see also French in America
Francis I (king of France) **1**:20, 24
Franklin, Benjamin
1775 **1**:88
almanacs **2**:42
Constitutional Convention **2**:33
E Pluribus Unum **2**:5
Independence National Historical Park **2**:9
Paris, Treaty of **2**:29
Paxton Boys **1**:77
Pennsylvania Gazette **1**:68
Franks, Bobby **6**:38
fraud *see* ethics and corruption
Frawley, William **7**:79
Fredericksburg, Battle of **3**:95
freedom of religion **1**:44, 78; **8**:21
freedom of speech **2**:51; **5**:7
freedom of the press **1**:71; **2**:51; **3**:23; **8**:63
Freedom Summer murders **8**:34
Free French government **7**:39
Freeman, Daniel **4**:34
Freer Gallery **3**:45
Frelinghuysen, Theodorus **1**:67
Frémont, John C. **3**:32, 66
French and Indian War **1**:72
1755 **1**:74
Ojibwe (Chippewa) **1**:73
Paxton Boys **1**:77
Washington, George **2**:38
French in America
Cadillac, Antoine de la Mothe **1**:60
Fort Rosalie **1**:68
Marquette and Jolliet **1**:54
Nicolet, Jean **1**:52
Ribaut, Jean **1**:29
Frick, Henry Clay **5**:6
Friends, Society of *see* Quakers
Friendship 7 (spacecraft) **8**:21
Frigidaire **5**:84
frontier *see* pioneer life; West, The
"front porch" campaign of McKinley **5**:23
frozen foods **6**:27; **7**:70
Fugitive Slave Act **3**:59
Fulton, Robert **2**:65
fur trade **1**:59, 60; **2**:68, 86, 87
F.W. Woolworth Company **9**:80

G

Gable, Clark **6**:87
Gadsden, James **3**:64
Gadsden Purchase **3**:63, 64
Gagarin, Yuri **8**:19
Gage, Thomas **1**:92
gag rules **3**:16
Gall **4**:63

Galveston (Texas) **3**:69
gambling **1**:73; **6**:18
games *see* gambling; toys and games
Gandil, Chick **6**:18
gangsters *see* organized crime
Garfield, James A. **4**:56, 71, 72
Garrett, Patrick **4**:74
Garrett, Robert **5**:21
gasoline **7**:16; **8**:72
Gast, John **3**:41
Gates, Horatio **2**:18
Gatsby, Jay **6**:39
Gaynor, Gloria **8**:79
Gehrig, Lou **6**:85, 86
Gemini missions **8**:36, 39
General Electric Company **6**:85
General Slocum disaster **5**:52
Genêt, Edmond **2**:45
genetic engineering **9**:73
Geological Survey, U.S. **4**:53
George II (king of England) **1**:68
George III (king of England) **1**:81, 87; **2**:29
George VI (king of England) **6**:69
Georgetown University **9**:71
Georgia
1825 **2**:89
Chickamauga, Battle of **4**:14
hurricane Hugo **9**:15
Kennesaw Mountain, Battle of **4**:24
Martin Luther King, Jr., National Historic Site **6**:52
Olympic Games (1996) **9**:60
Second Continental Congress **1**:93
settlement of **1**:69
Sherman's March to the Sea **4**:26
tornadoes (1998) **9**:94
Trail of Tears **3**:24
Germany **7**:65; **8**:29; **9**:19
see also World War I; World War II
Geronimo **4**:87
Gershwin, George **6**:74
Gettysburg, Battle of **4**:5, 10
Gettysburg Address **3**:81; **4**:16; **6**:31
Gettysburg National Military Park **4**:11
geysers **4**:55
Ghana, Clinton's visit to **9**:92
Ghost **9**:19
Ghost Dance **4**:95, 96
G.I. Bill **7**:33, 43
Gibson, Charles Dana **6**:6
Gibson, J.L. **5**:48
Gibson, Robert "Hoot" **9**:44
Gilbert Islands, Battle of the **7**:31
Gillette, King C. **5**:20
Gingrich, Newt **9**:38
Girl Scouts **5**:77
Glackens, William **5**:80
Glen Canyon Dam **9**:55
Glenn, John H., Jr. **8**:21
Glidden, Joseph **4**:58
Gloria **8**:65
Glory **4**:12
Goddard, Robert **6**:41; **8**:8
Godey, Louis **3**:10
Godey's Lady's Book **3**:10
Godspeed (ship) **1**:37, 39
Golden Hind (ship) **1**:32
gold **1**:10, 25
Golden Gate Bridge **6**:81
Golden Hind (ship) **1**:32
golden spike **4**:46
Goldman, Ronald **9**:34, 40, 65
gold rushes
California **3**:51, 53, 54, 55
Colorado **3**:73
Klondike Gold Rush National Historical Park **5**:26
golf, early days of **5**:78
Gompers, Samuel **4**:89
Gone With the Wind **6**:85, 87
Goodman, Andrew **8**:34
Goodman, Benny **6**:29, 76
Goodspeed (ship) *see Godspeed*

Goodyear, Charles **3**:27
Goodyear Tire & Rubber Company **3**:27
GOP *see* Republican Party
Gorbachev, Mikhail **9**:21
Gordon, Gary L. **4**:7
Gore, Al **9**:23, 31, 69, 75
Goree Island (Senegal) **9**:92
Goren, Charles **6**:63
Gorman, Margaret **6**:26
Gorrie, John **5**:84
Gorson, Aaron H. **5**:40
Gosnold, Bartholomew **1**:35
Gossett, Louis, Jr. **8**:81
government, federal
    Bill of Rights **2**:41
    Constitution, ratification of the **2**:35
    shutdown (1995) **9**:37
    Washington (D.C.) **2**:52
Gramm, Phil **9**:54
Grammy Awards **9**:41
Grand Canyon National Park **1**:26; **4**:53; **9**:55
Grand Coulee Dam **6**:94
Grand Forks (North Dakota) **9**:67, 68
Grand Old Party *see* Republican Party
Grange, Red **4**:47
Granger movement **4**:61
Grant, Cary **7**:56
Grant, Ulysses S. **4**:5, 18, 27, 39, 45
    Appomattox Court House **4**:29
    Chattanooga, Battle of **4**:15
    Credit Mobilier scandal **4**:56
    Petersburg, Siege of **4**:22
    Richmond **4**:28
    Shiloh, Battle of **3**:89
    Spotsylvania, Battle of **4**:21
    Vicksburg, Siege of **4**:9
    West Point **2**:58
    Wilderness, Battle of the **4**:20
Grapes of Wrath, The **6**:57
Gray, Robert **2**:43
Great Awakening **1**:67
Great Britain
    1765 **1**:81
    Atlantic Charter **6**:92
    French and Indian War **1**:72
    Marshall Plan **7**:68
    Paris, Treaty of **2**:29
    Potsdam Conference **7**:53
    slave trade, end of the **2**:65
    war brides **7**:56
    see also Revolutionary War; War of 1812
Great Flood of 1993 **9**:31
Great Gatsby, The **6**:39
Great Lakes **5**:40; **8**:5
Great Migration **1**:49
Great Molasses Disaster **6**:20
Great Plains **1**:11; **2**:81; **4**:34, 35
Great Serpent Mound **1**:6
Great Society **8**:32, 40
Great Train Robbery, The **5**:50
Great White Fleet **5**:58
Green, Andy **9**:83
Green, Ernest **7**:93
Green Berets **9**:35
Greene, Nathanael **2**:26, 27
Greenland **5**:65
Green Mountain Boys **1**:96; **2**:6
Greensboro (North Carolina) **8**:9
Greenwood, Isaac **1**:68
Grenada, invasion of **9**:6
Griffith, D.W. **4**:41
Grissom, Virgil "Gus" **8**:39, 45
Groves, Leslie R. **7**:52
Guadalcanal, Battle of **7**:21, 29, 30
Guadalupe Hidalgo, Treaty of **3**:53
Guam **5**:28, 36; **7**:33, 37; **9**:91
Guerrière (British ship) **2**:50, 70
guerrillas **4**:17
Guilford Courthouse, Battle of **2**:27
Guinness, Alec **8**:84
Guiteau, Charles Julius **4**:72
Gulf War *see* Persian Gulf War
Gulick, Luther Halsey **3**:60
guns **3**:20; **4**:50; **8**:93

gymnastics **9**:61

H

Haiti, U.S. troops in **9**:35
Hale, Alan **9**:74
Hale, Nathan **2**:11
Hale, Sarah **3**:10
Hale-Bopp, Comet **9**:68, 74
Haley, Alex **8**:81
Half Moon (ship) **1**:40
Hamill, Mark **8**:84
Hamilton, Alexander **2**:33, 34, 40, 55, 63
Hamilton, Andrew **1**:71
Hammerstein, Oscar, II **6**:48; **7**:32
Hancock, John **1**:85, 89, 93; **2**:7
handicapped people *see* disabled people
Handler, Ruth **8**:7
Hanford (Washington) **7**:52
Harding, Warren G. **6**:21, 25, 32, 33, 34, 35
Harlan, John Marshall **5**:22
Harlem Renaissance **6**:36
Harpers Ferry (West Virginia) **3**:73
Harpers Ferry National Historical Park **3**:74
Harrison, Benjamin **3**:29; **4**:92
    Erie, Lake, Battle of **2**:72
    Harrison, Benjamin **4**:92
    log cabins **1**:51
    Thames, Battle of the **2**:73
    Tippecanoe, Battle of **2**:69
    Tyler, John **3**:30
Harrison, George **8**:33
Harrison, Peter **1**:78
Harrison, William Henry **3**:29
    Erie, Lake, Battle of **2**:72
    Harrison, Benjamin **4**:92
    log cabins **1**:51
    Thames, Battle of the **2**:73
    Tippecanoe, Battle of **2**:69
    Tyler, John **3**:30
Hartford (Connecticut) **3**:20
Harvard University **1**:53, 65
Hastings, Lansford **3**:47
Hatfields and McCoys **4**:77
Hauptmann, Bruno Richard **6**:64, 73
Hawaii
    1893 revolution **5**:9
    1898 **5**:27
    Cook, James **2**:22
    50th anniversary of end of World War II **9**:48
    Keck telescopes **9**:32
    Manifest Destiny **3**:41
    Pearl Harbor **6**:96
    U.S. annexation of **5**:35
Hawaii, University of **9**:32
"hawks" (supporters of Vietnam War) **8**:38
Hay, John M. **5**:28; **9**:91
Hayes, Lucy Webb **4**:67
Hayes, Mary Ludwig *see* Pitcher, Molly
Hayes, Rutherford B. **4**:62, 66, 67, 68
Haymarket Riot **4**:85, 86
health *see* medicine and health
Hearst, Patty **8**:75
Hearst, William Randolph **6**:95
Heiden, Eric **8**:89
Hemingway, Ernest **4**:83
Hendrix, Jimi **8**:57
Henri, Robert **5**:80
Henried, Paul **7**:19
Henry, Patrick **1**:79, 80, 81, 87, 88
Henson, Jim **8**:58
Henson, Matthew **5**:65, 66
Hermitage, the **3**:14
Herold, David **4**:33
Hessians **2**:14, 15
Hewitt, Don **8**:51
Heyward, DuBose **6**:74
Hickok, Wild Bill **3**:20
Hill, Larry **9**:52
Hinckley, John W., Jr. **8**:91, 93
Hindenburg disaster **6**:79, 82
hippies **8**:57
Hiroshima (Japan) **7**:52, 54
Hirshhorn Museum and Sculpture Garden **3**:45
Hispaniola **1**:19

historic preservation
    Martin Luther King, Jr., National Historic Site **6**:52
historic restorations/re-enactments
    Harpers Ferry National Historical Park **3**:74
    Jamestown Festival Park **1**:39
    Minute Man National Historical Park **1**:91
    Plimoth Plantation **1**:46
    Williamsburg (Virginia) **1**:50
Hitchcock, Alfred **7**:82
Hitler, Adolf **6**:79; **7**:50; **9**:73
hockey *see* ice hockey
Hodges, Courtney **7**:48
Hoffman, Dustin **7**:72
holidays
    Earth Day **8**:61
    Flag Day **8**:15
    Jefferson Davis' birthday **3**:83
    Thanksgiving **1**:47
Holland (submarine) **5**:38
Holland, Clifford M. **6**:47
Holland, John Philip **5**:38
Holland Tunnel **6**:47
Holmes, Oliver Wendell **2**:50
Homestead Act **4**:34
homesteaders **5**:9
Homestead Strike **5**:6
Home to Harlem **6**:36
Hooker, Joseph **4**:8
Hoover, Herbert **6**:50, 51, 58, 65
Hoover, J. Edgar **8**:66
Hoover, Lou **6**:51
Hoover Dam **6**:59
Hopi Indians **1**:6, 13, 23
Hornet (aircraft carrier) **7**:7, 13
Horowitz, Vladimir **8**:41
horror movies **7**:82
horses **1**:11; **2**:91
Horseshoe Bend National Military Park **2**:75
hostages
    Iran **8**:80, 87, 88, 91; **9**:12
    Olympic Games (1972) **8**:68
hotels **3**:5, 73; **6**:49
hot line (U.S.–USSR) **8**:25
Hour of Gold, Hour of Lead **6**:64
House of Representatives, U.S.
    1800 election decision **2**:55
    1994 **9**:34
    Buchanan, James **3**:71
    Bush, George **9**:16
    Davis, Jefferson **3**:83
    Ferraro, Geraldine **9**:9
    gag rules **3**:16
    Garfield, James A. **4**:71
    Kennedy, John F. **8**:16
    McKinley, William **5**:23
housing
    Levittowns **7**:62
    log cabins **1**:51
    Monsanto House of the Future **4**:43
    Samoan thatch houses **5**:39
    sod houses **4**:35
Houston, Sam **3**:17, 18
Hovenden, Thomas **3**:73
Howe, Elias **3**:44
Howe, William **2**:10
How Green Was My Valley **6**:95
How the Other Half Lives **4**:95
Hubble, Edwin P. **9**:20
Hubble Space Telescope **9**:20, 62
Hudson, Henry **1**:40
Hudson Bay **1**:40
Hudson River **1**:40; **2**:65, 94
Hudson River School **2**:94
Hughes, Langston **6**:36
Hugo (hurricane) **9**:15
Hula-Hoops **7**:96
Hull, Isaac **2**:50
human rights **7**:55
Humphrey, Hubert H. **8**:47
hunting and trapping **2**:30, 86; **4**:42; **5**:88
Huntress, Wesley **9**:84
Hurricane Express, The **5**:79

hurricanes **9**:15, 23, 25
Hurston, Zora Neale **6**:36
Hussein, Saddam **9**:19, 22, 64, 90
"Hustle, The" (song) **8**:79
Hyatt, John **4**:43
Hyde Park (New York) **6**:69
hydrogen bombs **7**:34, 73, 81; **8**:11

I

ice-cream cones **5**:51
iced tea **5**:51
ice hockey **5**:48; **8**:89; **9**:88
Iceland **7**:68
icemen **5**:84
ice skating **8**:89; **9**:89
"If this be treason, make the most of it" **1**:81
"I have a dream" **6**:31; **8**:31
Illinois **2**:36; **3**:12, 36, 72; **6**:45
    see also Chicago
I Love Lucy **7**:79
immigration **1**:44; **4**:34, 88; **5**:8; **6**:19
impeachment of Andrew Johnson **4**:32, 39, 40
Incan Empire **1**:27
Inchon, landing at **7**:75
income tax **5**:82; **6**:44; **7**:21
indentured servants **1**:43
Independence (Missouri) **2**:83
Independence Day *see* Fourth of July
Independence Hall **2**:9
Independence National Historical Park **2**:8, 9
Indiana **2**:36, 69, 92; **3**:29
Indian-head nickel **4**:42
Indians, American *see* Native Americans
industrial revolution **3**:19
influenza epidemic (1918) **6**:5, 16
Inouye, Daniel **7**:27
insurance **6**:75; **8**:40
integration *see* desegregation
intercontinental ballistic missiles (ICBMs) **7**:58
Interior, U.S. Department of the **6**:34
Internal Revenue Service **5**:82
international law **7**:55
interstate commerce **7**:78
Intolerable Acts **1**:87
inventions and inventors
    air conditioners **5**:47
    barbed wire **4**:58
    Bell, Alexander Graham **4**:64
    Birdseye's frozen foods **6**:27
    Borden's condensed milk **3**:69
    Burroughs adding machine **5**:11
    Bushnell's submarine *Turtle* **2**:12
    Carlson, Chester **6**:84
    cash registers **4**:69
    cog railways **4**:49
    Colt's revolver **3**:20
    compact discs **9**:7
    computers **7**:59
    Cooper's *Tom Thumb* **3**:9
    cotton gin **2**:48
    Curtiss, Glenn **5**:73
    Deere's steel plow **3**:26
    De Forest, Lee **5**:69
    Edison, Thomas Alva **9**:72
    FM radio **6**:62
    Fulton's steamboat **2**:65
    Gillette's razor **5**:20
    Goddard, Robert **6**:41
    Goodyear, Charles **3**:27
    Holland's submarine **5**:38
    Howe, Elias **3**:44
    Langley, Samuel **5**:25
    lasers **8**:13
    Lawrence, Ernest O. **6**:54
    McCormick Reaper **3**:15
    Mergenthaler, Otto **4**:81
    microwave ovens **8**:46
    Monticello **1**:83
    Otis, Elisha **3**:67
    phonograph **4**:68
    plastics **4**:43
    Polaroid camera **7**:64

inventions and inventors (cont.)
    Pullman's sleeping car **4:**36
    Remington typewriter **4:**59
    telegraph **3:**37
    transistors **7:**69
    Westinghouse, George **4:**51
    Winchester rifle **4:**50
    Wright, Orville and Wilbur **5:**49
    zippers **5:**14
"I only regret that I have but one life
    to lose for my country" **2:**11
Iowa **9:**85
Iran **8:**87, 91; **9:**12
Iran-contra affair **8:**92; **9:**12, 13
Iranian hostage crisis **8:**80, 87, 88
Iraq **9:**19, 21, 22, 64, 90
Irish in America **3:**48; **4:**46
iron and steel industry **5:**40
"Iron Horse" **6:**86
Iroquois **1:**24
Irving, Washington **2:**80
Irwin, Jim **8:**64
Isabella (queen of Spain) **1:**16
Ishmael (fictional character) **3:**61
isolationism **6:**79
Israel **8:**85
Italy **7:**9, 25, 26, 35, 36
Ives, James Merritt *see* Currier &
    Ives
I Was a Male War Bride **7:**56
Iwo Jima, Battle of **7:**47

J

Jackson, Andrew **2:**89; **3:**5, 6, 16
    Bank of the United States **3:**8
    Eaton, Peggy **3:**7
    Florida **2:**82
    Hermitage, the **3:**14
    Horseshoe Bend **2:**75
    New Orleans, Battle of **2:**76
    Polk, James K. **3:**38
    Seminole Wars **2:**79
    Van Buren, Martin **3:**22
    War of 1812 **2:**71
Jackson, Jesse **9:**50
Jackson, Rachel **3:**14
Jackson, "Shoeless" Joe **6:**18
Jackson, Stonewall **3:**90, 91; **4:**8
Jackson, William Henry **3:**33
Jackson State College **8:**59
James, Willy **9:**70
Jamestown (Virginia)
    1619 **1:**42
    Bacon's Rebellion **1:**55, 56
    founding of **1:**37
    Gosnold, Bartholomew **1:**35
    Jamestown Festival Park **1:**39
    Smith, John **1:**38
Jamestown Festival Park **1:**39
Jamison, Herbert **5:**21
Japan
    Great White Fleet **5:**58
    opening of **2:**72; **3:**58, 65
    Russo-Japanese War **5:**53
    World War II apology **9:**48
    see also World War II
Japanese in America **7:**5, 20, 27
Jarvis, Gregory B. **9:**11
Java (British ship) **2:**71
Jay, John **2:**29, 34
jazz **6:**29, 76
Jazz Age **6:**39
Jazz Singer, The **6:**44
Jeeps **7:**28
Jefferson, Thomas **2:**45, 56, 61
    1800 election decision **2:**55
    Alien and Sedition Acts **2:**51
    Barbary Wars **2:**57
    Bill of Rights **2:**41
    Declaration of Independence
        1:93; **2:**7
    E Pluribus Unum **2:**5
    Harpers Ferry **3:**74
    Library of Congress **2:**54
    Monroe, James **2:**78
    Monticello **1:**83
    Mount Rushmore **6:**93
    public education **5:**12
    quoted on bald eagle **2:**30

Washington, George **2:**38
William and Mary, College of
    1:63
Jeffersons, The **8:**65
jetliners **8:**8
Jews in America **1:**78; **7:**57
John Paul II (pope) **9:**49
Johns, Jasper **8:**26
Johnson, Andrew **4:**27, 32
    Alaska, purchase of **4:**38
    impeachment **4:**39, 40
    Lincoln's assassination **4:**30, 33
Johnson, Henry **6:**7
Johnson, James Weldon **6:**36
Johnson, Lady Bird **8:**32
Johnson, Lyndon Baines **8:**32, 47
    DaNang, landing at **8:**38
    King assassination, quoted on
        8:50
    Ku Klux Klan investigation **4:**41
    Medicare and Medicaid **8:**40
    Pueblo incident **8:**49
    Selma-to-Montgomery marches
        8:37
    Warren Commission Report
        8:35
Johnson, Magic **9:**26
Johnson, Philip (originator of Navajo
    Code Talkers) **7:**10
Johnston, Albert Sidney **3:**89
Johnston, Joseph E. **3:**88, 91; **4:**24
Johnstown flood **4:**93
Joint Chiefs of Staff **9:**46
Jolliet, Louis **1:**54
Jolson, Al **6:**44
Jones, John Paul **3:**39
Jones, Paula **9:**96
Jones, Reca **1:**5
Jordan, Michael **9:**26
Jorgensen, John **7:**60
journalism
    60 Minutes **8:**51
    see also newspapers; press,
        freedom of the
judges *see* Supreme Court
Judson, Whitcomb L. **5:**14
June Bug (airplane) **5:**73
Jungle, The **5:**56
Justice, U.S. Department of **6:**19,
    34; **8:**63

K

kachinas **1:**13
Kaczynski, Theodore **9:**56
Kaiser, Henry J. **6:**94
Kamehameha I **5:**35
Kanagawa, Treaty of **3:**65
Kansas **3:**68
Kansas-Nebraska Act **3:**63, 66, 68
Kasserine Pass, Battle of the **7:**24
KDKA (radio station) **6:**35
Kearney, Stephen **3:**43
Kearsarge (warship) **4:**23
Keck telescopes **9:**32
Kefauver, Estes **7:**78
Kefauver Crime Commission **7:**78
Kellogg, John H. **5:**42
Kellogg, Will **5:**42
Kelly, Grace **7:**90
Kelly, Oliver H. **4:**61
Kelly, William **5:**40
Kennedy, Jacqueline **2:**53; **8:**32
Kennedy, John F. **8:**16
    assassination **8:**28
    Bay of Pigs invasion **8:**18
    Berlin visit **8:**29
    Clinton, Bill **9:**28
    Cuban missile crisis **8:**21, 25
    Gemini missions **8:**36
    Johnson, Lyndon Baines **8:**32
    Kennedy-Nixon debates **8:**14
    Mississippi, University of,
        desegregation **8:**21
    Peace Corps **8:**17
    promise to land men on the
        moon **8:**53
    Shepard, Alan, first American in
        space **8:**19

Warren Commission Report
    8:35
Kennedy, Robert F. **8:**47, 52
Kennedy-Nixon debates **8:**14
Kennesaw Mountain, Battle of **4:**24
Kennesaw Mountain National
    Battlefield Park **4:**24
Kent, Rockwell **3:**61
Kent State killings **8:**59, 60, 62
Kentucky **3:**94; **4:**77; **6:**45; **9:**94
Kern, Jerome **5:**59; **6:**48
Kettle Hill **5:**33
Key, Francis Scott **2:**71
Keyes, Alan **9:**54
Keystone Kops **5:**50
Khobar Towers (Dhahran, Saudi
    Arabia) **9:**58
Khomeini, Ayatollah Ruhollah **8:**87
Khrushchev, Nikita **8:**12, 21, 25
kidnappings **6:**38, 64, 73; **8:**75
Kilrain, Jake **4:**76
King, Coretta Scott **6:**52; **8:**50
King, Martin Luther, Jr. **8:**47
    assassination **8:**50
    Lincoln Memorial **6:**31
    march on Washington **8:**31
    Martin Luther King, Jr., National
        Historic Site **6:**52
    Montgomery bus boycott **7:**89,
        90
    Selma-to-Montgomery marches
        8:37
King, Rodney **9:**23, 24
"King and Queen Surrounded by
    Swift Nudes, The" **5:**83
King Philip's War **1:**55
King's Mountain, Battle of **2:**24
King William's War **1:**61
Kinte, Kunta **8:**81
Kitty Hawk (North Carolina) **5:**49
Klondike Gold Rush National
    Historical Park **5:**26
Knowlton's Rangers **2:**11
Know-Nothing Party **3:**58
Knox, Henry **2:**6
Kodak camera **4:**91
Korea **8:**49
Korean War **7:**73, 74, 76, 81
    desegregation of the armed
        forces **7:**67; **9:**87
    Inchon, landing at **7:**75
    MacArthur, Douglas, fired by
        Truman **7:**77
    Strategic Air Command **7:**58
    Truman, Harry S. **7:**45
    Westmoreland, William **8:**48
Koresh, David **9:**30
Krause, Allison **8:**62
Kroft, Steve **8:**51
Kukla, Fran, and Ollie **7:**76
Ku Klux Klan **4:**41; **8:**34
Kunstler, Mort **4:**18, 21
Kurds **9:**64
Kuwait **9:**19, 21, 22
Kwan, Michelle **9:**89

L

labor issues
    child labor **4:**57
    Haymarket Riot **4:**86
    labor unions **4:**89; **6:**19
    Rosie the Riveter **7:**17
    Social Security Act **6:**75
    welfare reform **9:**63
    WPA **6:**78
    see also strikes
Ladd, Alan **6:**39
Laettner, Christian **9:**26
Lafayette, Marquis de **2:**31
Lafayette Escadrille **5:**91
Lafitte, Jean **2:**76
Lake Erie, Battle of **2:**72, 73; **3:**65
Lake George, Battle of **1:**74
Lamb, William F. **6:**58
Land, Edwin H. **7:**64
land rush **4:**34, 94; **5:**9
landscape painting **2:**94
Lane, F.A. **5:**21
Lane, Harriet **3:**71

Langley (aircraft carrier) **5:**25; **7:**13
Langley, Samuel **5:**25
Langston, John Mercer **3:**13
Lansing, Robert **5:**96
Lansky, Meyer "Socks" **7:**78
LaSalle, Eriq **9:**36
La Salle, Sieur de **1:**58, 59
lasers **8:**13
"Last Moments of John Brown, The"
    3:73
Latter-day Saints *see* Mormons
law
    church arson **9:**52
    colonial punishments **1:**57
    Constitution, ratification of the
        2:35
    Fugitive Slave Act **3:**59
    G.I. Bill **7:**43
    Medicare and Medicaid **8:**40
    Miranda decision **8:**42
    Nuremberg trials **7:**57
    Pure Food and Drug Act **5:**56
    Scopes trial **6:**40
    Simpson, O.J., civil trial **9:**65
    Social Security Act **6:**75
    United Nations **7:**55
    see also police; Supreme Court
Lawrence (ship) **2:**72
Lawrence, D.H. **1:**41
Lawrence, Ernest O. **6:**54
Lawrence, James **2:**46
Lazarus, Emma **4:**88
Leach, Archie *see* Grant, Cary
League of Nations **5:**81; **6:**5, 15, 21
Lear, Norman **8:**65
Lebanon **7:**95; **9:**5
LeClerc, Jacques **7:**39
Lee, Charles **2:**23
Lee, Ezra **2:**12
Lee, "Mother Ann" **3:**46
Lee, Robert E. **4:**5, 18, 27
    Antietam, Battle of **3:**92, 93
    Appomattox Court House **4:**29
    Bull Run, Second Battle of **3:**90
    Chancellorsville, Battle of **4:**8
    Fredericksburg, Battle of **3:**95
    Gettysburg, Battle of **4:**10, 11
    Harpers Ferry **3:**74
    Mexico City, capture of **3:**50
    Peninsular Campaign **3:**88
    Petersburg, Siege of **4:**22
    Richmond (Virginia) **4:**28
    Spotsylvania, Battle of **4:**21
    West Point **2:**58
    Wilderness, Battle of the **4:**20
"Legend of Sleepy Hollow, The" **2:**80
legends and folklore
    Chicago fire (1871) and Mrs.
        O'Leary's cow **4:**54
    fountain of youth **1:**19
    Ross, Betsy, and American flag
        8:15
    Thunderbird myth **7:**88
    Titanic band selection **5:**75
Legion of Merit **7:**9
Lehman, Herbert H. **6:**37
Leigh, Vivien **6:**87
L'Enfant, Pierre Charles **2:**52
Lennon, John **8:**33, 88, 90
Leonov, Aleksei **8:**39, 76
Leopold, Nathan **6:**38
Levin, Ira **9:**73
Levin, Meyer **6:**38
Levittowns **7:**62
Lewinsky, Monica **9:**96
Lewis, Carl **9:**8
Lewis, Meriwether **2:**62
Lewis, Robert **7:**54
Lewis and Clark expedition **2:**62
Lexington (aircraft carrier) **7:**13
Lexington (Massachusetts) **1:**88, 89,
    90, 91
Leyte Gulf, Battle of **7:**33, 41
Liberty, Statue of **4:**85, 88; **8:**77
Liberty Bell **2:**8, 9
Liberty bonds **6:**6
libraries **2:**54; **4:**52
Library of Congress **2:**54
Lichtenstein, Roy **8:**26

life on other planets **8**:78; **9**:78
Life on the Mississippi **2**:93
lighthouses **3**:84
Liliuokalani (queen of Hawaii) **5**:9, 35
Lin, Maya **8**:96
Lincoln, Abraham **3**:78, 80, 81, 86; **4**:5, 18, 27
  assassination **4**:30, 31, 33
  Black Hawk War **3**:12
  Emancipation Proclamation **4**:6
  Fredericksburg, Battle of **3**:95
  Frémont, John C. **3**:32
  Gettysburg **4**:11
  Gettysburg Address **4**:16
  Grant, Ulysses S. **4**:45
  Kentucky **3**:94
  Lincoln-Douglas debates **3**:72
  Lincoln Memorial **6**:31
  Mount Rushmore **6**:93
  Pacific Railway Act **4**:46
  Republican Party **3**:66
  Richmond (Virginia) **4**:28
  secret arrival in Washington **3**:82
  South Carolina, secession of **3**:79
  Thanksgiving **1**:47
Lincoln, Benjamin **2**:28
Lincoln Bedroom (White House) **9**:77
Lincoln-Douglas debates **3**:72
Lincoln Memorial **6**:31, 85; **8**:31
Lindbergh, Anne Morrow **6**:64
Lindbergh, Charles **6**:43, 44, 46, 64
Lindbergh kidnapping **6**:64, 73
Linotype machine **4**:81
Lipinski, Tara **9**:68, 89
literature
  Adventures of Huckleberry Finn **4**:83
  Harlem Renaissance **6**:36
  Moby-Dick **3**:61
  see also poetry; theater
Little America **6**:42
Little Bighorn, Battle of **4**:62, 63
Little Egypt (belly dancer) **5**:10
Little Rock (Arkansas) **7**:92, 93
Little Women **4**:39
Livingston, Robert **2**:65
loans, government **7**:43
Lockheed P-80 **8**:8
locks, canal **2**:91
Loeb, Richard **6**:38
log cabins **1**:51; **4**:71
Loman, Willy **7**:72
Lone Ranger, The **6**:35
Long, Crawford **3**:31
Long, Stephen H. **2**:81
Longfellow, Henry Wadsworth **1**:74, 89
Long Island, Battle of **2**:5, 10
Longs Peak **2**:81
Lookout Mountain **4**:15
Looney, Shelley **9**:88
Los Angeles (California)
  1781 **2**:25
  1992 **9**:23
  1994 **9**:34
  Manson murders **8**:56
  riots (1992) **9**:24
  Simpson, O.J., trials **9**:40, 65
Los Angeles Dodgers **7**:80
Lost Colony **1**:33, 34
Louganis, Greg **9**:8
Lou Gehrig's disease **6**:85, 86
Louis, Joe **6**:90
Louis-Dreyfus, Julia **9**:95
Louisiana
  1682 **1**:58
  1819 **2**:80
  Cadillac, Antoine de la Mothe **1**:60
  Cajuns **1**:74
  hurricane Andrew **9**:25
  Mississippi River flood (1927) **6**:45
  plantations **2**:60
  Plessy v. *Ferguson* **5**:22

Watson Brake Mounds **1**:5
Louisiana Purchase **1**:59; **2**:56, 61, 62, 64
Louisiana Purchase Exposition **5**:51
Lovejoy, Elijah **3**:23
Lovejoy, Owen **3**:23
Low, Juliette Gordon **5**:77
Lowell, Francis **3**:19
Lowell National Historical Park **3**:19
Loyalists **2**:24
Lucas, George **8**:84
Lucas, John **7**:35
Ludlow Massacre **5**:87
Lufbery, Raoul **5**:91
Luks, George **5**:80
Lunar Roving Vehicle **8**:64
Lusitania (ship) **5**:89
Luzon Island **7**:6
Lyon, Matthew **2**:51

M

MacArthur, Douglas **7**:76
  Bonus Army **6**:61
  Inchon, landing at **7**:75
  Korean War **7**:74
  Leyte Gulf, Battle of **7**:41
  quoted on Marine Corps **1**:95
  Truman, Harry S. **7**:77
Madison, Dolley **2**:9, 53, 74
Madison, James **2**:33, 34, 41, 67, 74
Madison Square Garden (New York City) **5**:57
Mad magazine **5**:18
Magellan, Ferdinand **5**:36
magnetrons **8**:46
mah-jongg **6**:28
Mahone, Paula **9**:85
Maiman, Theodore **8**:13
Maine **2**:80
Maine, USS, sinking of the **5**:27, 28, 29; **9**:91
Majuro Atoll **7**:34
Makin **7**:31
malaria **2**:52
Malone, Karl **9**:26
Manassas, Battles of *see* Bull Run, First Battle of; Bull Run, Second Battle of
Manassas National Battlefield Park **3**:91
Mandela, Nelson **9**:19, 92
Manhattan Island **1**:48
Manhattan Project **7**:15, 52, 59
Manifest Destiny **3**:38, 41
Manila Bay, Battle of **5**:27, 30, 31
Mankiller, Wilma **1**:10
Manson, Charles **8**:56
Mantle, Mickey **8**:20
Marbury v. *Madison* **2**:61
March, Fredric **7**:72
Margulies, Julianna **9**:36
Mariana Islands, Battles of **7**:33, 37, 63
Marine Corps, U.S. **1**:95
  Barbary Wars **2**:57
  Belleau Wood, Battle of **6**:10
  bomb attack in Lebanon **9**:5
  DaNang, landing at **8**:38
  Gilbert Islands, Battle of the **7**:31
  Grenada, invasion of **9**:6
  Guadalcanal, Battle of **7**:30
  Haiti (1915) **9**:35
  Iwo Jima, Battle of **7**:47
  Los Angeles riots (1992) **9**:24
  Mariana Islands, Battles of **7**:37
  Marshall Islands, Battle of the **7**:34
  Naval Academy **3**:39
  Nicaragua **5**:67, 74
  O'Grady, Scott, rescue by **9**:43
  Okinawa, Battle of **7**:51
  Operation Desert Storm **9**:22
  Solomon Islands, Battle of the **7**:29
  Wake Island **6**:91
  women's units in World War II **7**:22
Maris, Roger **8**:20

Market-Garden, Operation **7**:40
Marne, First Battle of the **6**:12
Marne, Second Battle of the **6**:12
Marquette, Father Jacques **1**:54
marriage **3**:46; **7**:56
Mars **8**:77, 78; **9**:68, 79
Marsh, Sylvester **4**:49
Marshall, George C. **7**:68
Marshall, James **3**:54, 55
Marshall, Thurgood **7**:87
Marshall Field and Company **4**:44
Marshall Islands, Battle of the **7**:33, 34
Marshall Plan **7**:45, 68
Martha (passenger pigeon) **5**:88
Martha's Vineyard **1**:35
Martin Luther King, Jr., National Historic Site **6**:52
Maryland **1**:90; **3**:9, 39, 92; **8**:85
  see also Baltimore
Massachusetts
  1630 **1**:49
  1775 **1**:88
  Borden trial **5**:13
  Bunker Hill, Battle of **1**:92
  colonial punishments **1**:57
  Constitution, ratification of the **2**:35
  Coolidge, Calvin **6**:33
  Harvard College founding **1**:53
  Lowell National Historical Park **3**:19
  Minute Man National Historical Park **1**:91
  Minutemen **1**:90
  Pilgrims **1**:44
  Plimoth Plantation **1**:46
  public education **5**:12
  Revere, Paul **1**:89
  Sacco-Vanzetti case **6**:23
  Salem witch-hunt **1**:61, 62
  Shays' Rebellion **2**:31
  slavery **1**:43
  Utopian communities **2**:92
  whaling **2**:96
  see also Boston
Massasoit **1**:47, 55
mastodons **2**:55
Matisse, Henri **5**:83
Matsunaga, Spark **7**:27
Mattel, Inc. **8**:7
Matthew (ship) **1**:17
Maude **8**:65
Mauna Kea **9**:32
Mayflower (ship) **1**:44, 45
Mayflower II (ship) **1**:46
Mayflower Compact **1**:45
McAdoo, William G. **6**:6
McAuliffe, Anthony C. **7**:42
McAuliffe, Christa **9**:11
McCarthy, Joseph **7**:73, 86
McCartney, Bill **9**:82
McCartney, Paul **8**:33
McCaughey septuplets **9**:85
McClellan, George B. **3**:88, 90, 92, 93; **4**:18
McConnell, James **5**:91
McCormick, Cyrus **3**:15
McCormick, Robert **3**:85
McCormick Reaper **3**:15
McCoy, Van **8**:79
McCoy family **4**:77
McCulloch v. *Maryland* **2**:80
McDaniel, Hattie **6**:87
McDivitt, James A. **8**:39
McDowell, Irvin **3**:85, 91
McGuffey Readers **5**:12
McHenry, Fort **2**:71
McKay, Claude **6**:36
McKim, Mead & White **5**:57
McKinley, William **5**:23
  assassination **4**:72; **5**:43
  bicycles **5**:19
  Maine, USS, sinking of the **5**:29
  Spanish-American War **5**:28
  U.S. annexation of Hawaii **5**:35
McLaughlin, Pat **3**:76
McMurran, John T. **3**:40
McNair, Ronald E. **9**:11

McVeigh, Timothy J. **9**:42, 68, 76
Mead, Lake **6**:59
Meade, George G. **4**:10, 11
meat inspection **5**:56
Medal of Honor **4**:7; **6**:7; **9**:70
Medicare and Medicaid **8**:40
medicine and health
  anesthetics **3**:31
  Blackwell, Elizabeth **3**:55
  cloning **9**:73
  Coca-Cola **4**:90
  first open-heart surgery **5**:9
  first U.S. medical school **1**:81
  influenza epidemic **6**:16
  Lou Gehrig's disease **6**:85
  Medicare and Medicaid **8**:40
  polio, fight against **7**:83
  Pure Food and Drug Act (1906) **5**:54
  Red Cross **4**:75
  Reed, Walter **5**:34
Melrose Mansion **3**:40
Melville, Herman **3**:61
memorials *see* monuments and memorials
Mendaña Neyra, Alvaro de **7**:29
Menéndez de Avilés, Don Pedro **1**:31
men's rallies **9**:50, 82
Mercury program **8**:19
Meredith, James **8**:21, 24, 30
Mergenthaler, Otto **4**:81
mergers and acquisitions
  Walt Disney Company and ABC **9**:45
Merrimack (warship) **3**:86, 87
Merrimack River **3**:19
Mesa Verde National Park **1**:7, 9
Metacomet **1**:55
Methodists **1**:67
Meuse-Argonne offensive **6**:5, 14
Mexican War **3**:43, 48, 53
  Buena Vista, Battle of **3**:49
  Colt's revolver **3**:20
  Grant, Ulysses S. **4**:45
  Marine Corps **1**:95
  Mexico City, capture of **3**:50
  Polk, James K. **3**:38
  Taylor, Zachary **3**:56
Mexico
  1914 **5**:85
  Alamo, Battle of the **3**:16, 17
  Buena Vista, Battle of **3**:49
  Gadsden Purchase **3**:64
  Pershing chases Pancho Villa **5**:90
  San Jacinto, Battle of **3**:16, 18
  Zimmermann Telegram **5**:95
  see also Mexican War
Mexico City, capture of **3**:50
Michigan **1**:60; **2**:36; **8**:44
Michigan, Lake **1**:52
Micinsk, Jessica **9**:57
Micronesia **7**:63
microwave ovens **8**:46
Middle East **8**:72; **9**:19
midshipmen **3**:39
Midway, Battle of **7**:5, 12, 13
Midwestern U.S. flood **9**:31
military
  Air Force, U.S. **7**:61
  desegregation **7**:9, 67
  Medal of Honor **4**:7
  NATO **7**:71
  Navy, United States **2**:46
  Saudi Arabian bombing of U.S. troops **9**:58
  Selective Service Act **6**:89
  Sherman tanks **7**:8
  U.S. conflict with Iraq (1996) **9**:64
  women's units in World War II **7**:22
  see also branches of the U.S. armed forces
Military Academy, United States **2**:58; **3**:39; **8**:48
milk, condensed **3**:69
Miller, Arthur **1**:62; **7**:72

Miller, Glenn **6**:76
Miller, Jeffrey **8**:62
Miller, Shannon **9**:61
Miller, Zell **9**:94
"Million Man March" **9**:37, 50
Mills, Robert **4**:82
mill towns **3**:19
mining **3**:76; **5**:85, 87
Minneapolis-St. Paul (Minnesota) **3**:48
Minnesota **3**:48; **9**:67, 68
Minuit, Peter **1**:48
Minute Man National Historical Park **1**:91
minutemen **1**:88, 90, 91
Mir (space station) **9**:44
Miranda decision **8**:42
Miss America Pageant **6**:26
missiles *see* rockets and missiles
missing persons
    Earhart, Amelia **6**:79, 80
    Roanoke Island **1**:33, 34
Missionary Ridge **4**:15
missions, California **1**:82
Mississippi
    1819 **2**:80
    Freedom Summer murders **8**:34
    Jackson State College **8**:59
    Mississippi River flood (1927) **6**:45
    Natchez National Historical Park **3**:40
    Natchez Trace National Parkway **2**:59
    tornadoes (1998) **9**:94
    Vicksburg, Siege of **4**:9
Mississippi, University of **8**:21, 24
Mississippi River
    1541 **1**:26
    de Soto, Hernando **1**:27
    flood (1927) **6**:45
    Great Flood of 1993 **9**:31
    La Salle, Sieur de **1**:59
    Marquette and Jolliet **1**:54
    steamboats **2**:93
Missouri **2**:83; **3**:70; **6**:45
Missouri River **9**:31
Mitchell, Billy **7**:61
Mitchell, Margaret **6**:87
Mitsuru, Ushijima **7**:51
Mobile Bay, Battle of **4**:18
Moby-Dick **3**:61
Model T Ford **5**:60, 61
molasses **1**:64; **6**:20
Molly Pitcher *see* Pitcher, Molly
Mondale, Walter **8**:77; **9**:8, 9
Monitor (warship) **3**:86, 87
Monmouth, Battle of **2**:21, 23
Monroe, James **2**:15, 78, 80, 88
Monroe Doctrine **2**:78, 88, 90
Montana **4**:63
Monte Cassino, Battles for **7**:36
Montgomery (Alabama) **7**:89, 90; **8**:37
Montgomery, Bernard **7**:26
Montgomery, Richard **1**:94
Monticello **1**:83
Montreal (Quebec) **1**:24
monuments and memorials
    Gettysburg **4**:11
    Kent State killings **8**:62
    Lennon, John **8**:90
    Lincoln Memorial **6**:31
    Vietnam Veterans Memorial **8**:96
    Washington Monument **4**:82
    Wounded Knee, Battle of **4**:96
Moody, Helen Wills **4**:60
moon **8**:19, 45, 53, 55, 64, 76
Morgan, Daniel **2**:26
Morgan, William **3**:60
Morison, Samuel Eliot **3**:51
Mormons **3**:36, 48
Morocco **7**:14
Morrison, Marion Michael *see* Wayne, John
Morro, El (fort, Puerto Rico) **5**:32
Morro, El (rock, New Mexico) **1**:30

Morse, Samuel F.B. **3**:35, 37
Morse Code **3**:37
Morton, Thomas Green **3**:31
Mosby, John Singleton **4**:17, 25
Mosby's Rangers **4**:17, 25
Mother Teresa *see* Teresa, Mother
motion pictures *see* movies
Mott, Lucretia **3**:52
Moultrie, Fort **3**:84
Mound Builders **1**:5, 6
mountain men **2**:86, 87
Mount Rushmore **6**:93
Mount Vernon **1**:75
movies
    1933 **6**:67
    1939 **6**:85
    1941 **6**:90
    1990 **9**:19
    Birth of a Nation **4**:41
    Bonnie and Clyde **6**:66
    Bridge Too Far, A **7**:40
    Casablanca **7**:19
    Citizen Kane **6**:95
    early movies **5**:50
    Edison, Thomas Alva **5**:9
    E.T., the Extra-Terrestrial **8**:95
    Glory **4**:12
    Gone With the Wind **6**:87
    Great Gatsby, The **6**:39
    Hearst, Patty **8**:75
    I Was a Male War Bride **7**:56
    Jazz Singer, The **6**:44
    Porgy and Bess **6**:74
    serials **5**:79
    Star Wars trilogy **8**:84
    3-D movies **7**:82
    Titanic **9**:86
Mudd, Samuel **4**:33
mulberries (movable ports) **7**:38
mules **2**:91
Mullin, Chris **9**:26
Mullins, Priscilla **1**:45
multiple births **9**:85
Muppets **8**:58
Murayama, Tomiichi **9**:48
murder
    Billy the Kid **4**:74
    Bonnie and Clyde **6**:66
    Borden trial **5**:13
    Boston Strangler **8**:27
    Freedom Summer murders **8**:34
    Lennon, John **8**:88, 90
    Leopold and Loeb **6**:38
    Lindbergh kidnapping **6**:64
    Lovejoy, Elijah **3**:23
    Manson murders **8**:56
    Paxton Boys **1**:77
    Sacco-Vanzetti case **6**:23
    Selena **9**:41
    Simpson, O.J., case **9**:34, 37, 40, 65
    White, Stanford **5**:57
    see also assassinations
Murfreesboro, Battle of **3**:96
Murmansk (Russia) **6**:11
Murphy, Thomas S. **9**:45
Museum of the American Indian **3**:45
museums
    Cantigny, Battle of, in Illinois **6**:8
    Ellis Island **5**:8
    Ford's Theatre **4**:31
    Jamestown Festival Park **1**:39
    Natchez National Historical Park **3**:40
    Naval Academy **3**:39
    Shaker villages **3**:46
    Slater's mill in Pawtucket, Rhode Island **2**:39
    Smithsonian Institution **3**:45
    Strategic Air Command Museum **7**:58
music
    Beatles, the **8**:33
    big bands **6**:76
    disco dancing **8**:79
    Harlem Renaissance **6**:36
    jazz **6**:29
    Marine Corps Hymn **2**:57
    Porgy and Bess **6**:74

Selena **9**:41
    Woodstock Festival **8**:57
musical theater
    Oklahoma! **7**:32
    Porgy and Bess **6**:74
    Show Boat **6**:48
    Ziegfeld Follies **5**:59
My American Journey **9**:46

N

NAACP **5**:64; **7**:87; **8**:30
Nagasaki (Japan) **7**:52, 54
Naismith, James **3**:60; **5**:5
Napoleon I **2**:61
Nash, William **9**:51
Nashville (Tennessee) **3**:14; **9**:94
Nast, Thomas **2**:77
Natchez Indians **1**:68
Natchez National Historical Park **3**:40
Natchez Trace National Parkway **2**:59; **3**:40
National Aeronautics and Space Administration (NASA)
    Apollo 1 tragedy **8**:45
    Cassini space probe **9**:84
    Challenger disaster **9**:11
    Hubble Space Telescope **9**:62
    Lunar Roving Vehicle **8**:64
    Skylab **8**:71
    Viking Mars probes **8**:78
    weather satellites **8**:10
National Air and Space Museum **3**:45; **9**:37
National Archives **2**:41
National Association for the Advancement of Colored People **5**:64; **7**:87; **8**:30
national battlefields and battlefield parks **3**:91, 93, 96; **4**:24
National Broadcasting Company (NBC) **6**:35
National Cash Register Company **4**:69
National Gallery of Art **3**:45
National Guard **7**:92; **8**:37, 59, 62; **9**:24
national historical parks
    Appomattox Court House **4**:29
    Chaco Culture **1**:7
    Harpers Ferry **3**:74
    Independence **2**:9
    Klondike Gold Rush **5**:26
    Lowell **3**:19
    Minute Man **1**:91
    Natchez **3**:40
    San Antonio Missions **1**:70
    Valley Forge **2**:20
national historic landmarks **5**:66
national historic sites **4**:31; **5**:46; **6**:52, 69
National Hockey League **5**:48
national memorials **6**:93, 96
national military parks **2**:75; **4**:11
national monuments **1**:8, 28; **3**:84; **4**:34, 88; **9**:81
National Museum of Natural History **5**:88
national parks **1**:9; **4**:55, 95; **5**:45; **9**:14
national parkways **2**:59
National Recovery Administration **6**:83
National Republican Party **2**:89
National Youth Administration **6**:78
National Zoological Park **3**:45
native Americans
    Bacon's Rebellion **1**:56
    Black Hawk War **3**:12
    buffalo, decline of **4**:42
    California missions **1**:82
    Chaco Culture National Historical Park **1**:7
    Cherokee Nation **1**:10
    Code Talkers **7**:10
    Columbus, Christopher, controversy **9**:23
    Custer's Last Stand **4**:63
    French and Indian War **1**:72

Geronimo **4**:87
government guardianship (1871) **4**:54
Great Serpent Mound **1**:6
Hopi Indians **1**:13
Horseshoe Bend **2**:75
King Philip's War **1**:55
Manhattan Island **1**:48
Museum of the American Indian **3**:45
Navajo **1**:14
Nicolet, Jean, relationship with **1**:52
Northwest Ordinance **2**:36
Ojibwe (Chippewa) **1**:73
Paxton Boys, killed by **1**:77
Plains Indians **1**:11
Plimoth Plantation **1**:46
Pontiac's Rebellion **1**:76
Powell, John Wesley, worked to preserve culture **4**:53
Pueblo Indians **1**:23
reservations, relocated to **2**:89
Sacagawea **2**:62
San Antonio Missions National Historical Park **1**:70
Seminole Wars **2**:79
Taos **1**:41
Thanksgiving **1**:47
Thunderbird myth **7**:88
Tippecanoe, Battle of **2**:69
Trail of Tears **3**:24
War of 1812 **2**:71
Wounded Knee, Battle of **4**:95, 96
Wupatki National Monument **1**:8
NATO **7**:71; **9**:51
Nautilus (submarine) **7**:94, 95
Nauvoo (Illinois) **3**:36
Navajo **1**:14; **7**:10
Naval Academy, United States **2**:46; **3**:39
naval warfare
    Barbary Wars **2**:57
    Bushnell's submarine *Turtle* **2**:12
    Coral Sea, Battle of the **7**:11
    Erie, Lake, Battle of **2**:72
    Monitor vs. the *Merrimack* **3**:87
Navy, United States **2**:46
    Arthur, Chester Alan **4**:73
    captain played game of bridge for freedom of his ship **6**:63
    Coast Guard, U.S. **2**:40
    Coral Sea, Battle of the **7**:11
    Goddard, Robert **6**:41
    Great White Fleet **5**:58
    Kearsarge vs. the *Alabama* **4**:23
    Manila Bay, Battle of **5**:30
    Mariana Islands, Battles of **7**:37
    Naval Academy **3**:39
    Okinawa, Battle of **7**:51
    "Old Ironsides" **2**:50
    Pearl Harbor attack **6**:96
    Pueblo incident **8**:49
    submarines **5**:38
    War of 1812 **2**:70
    Wilkes expedition **3**:25
    women's units in World War II **7**:22
Nazis **6**:79; **7**:57
Neale, Thomas **1**:61
Nebraska **4**:34; **7**:58
Nelson, Gaylord **8**:61
Nelson, Lord **2**:57
Nesbit, Evelyn **5**:57
Netherlands **7**:40
Nevada **3**:73, 76; **6**:59
Nevins, Allan **4**:84
New Amsterdam **1**:40, 48
New Deal **6**:67
    Grand Coulee Dam **6**:94
    Roosevelt, Franklin D. **6**:68
    Social Security Act **6**:75
    Supreme Court **6**:83
    Tennessee Valley Authority **6**:72
    WPA **6**:78
New England **1**:38; **2**:44; **4**:52
Newfoundland **1**:12

New Guinea **7:**11
New Hampshire **1:**61, 90; **4:**13, 49
New Harmony (Indiana) **2:**92
New Haven (Connecticut) **1:**65; **3:**28; **4:**65
New Jersey
  Hindenburg disaster **6:**82
  Holland Tunnel **6:**47
  Lindbergh kidnapping **6:**64
  Miss America Pageant **6:**26
  Monmouth, Battle of **2:**23
  Princeton, Battle of **2:**17
  Trenton, Battle of **2:**15
  Washington crosses the Delaware **2:**14
  Wilson, Woodrow **5:**81
  women's suffrage **6:**24
New Mexico
  1846 **3:**43
  1912 **5:**74
  Chaco Culture National Historical Park **1:**7
  Estéban **1:**22
  Gadsden Purchase **3:**64
  Manhattan Project **7:**52
  Mexico City, capture of **3:**50
  Oñate, Juan de **1:**30
  Pueblo Indians **1:**23
  Roswell Incident **9:**78
  Santa Fe Trail **2:**83
  Taos **1:**41
New Netherland **1:**40
New Orleans (Louisiana) **1:**66; **2:**76
New Orleans (steamboat) **2:**93
New Orleans, Battle of **2:**71, 76; **3:**6
Newport (Rhode Island) **1:**78
newspapers **1:**68; **5:**18
New York
  dance marathons **6:**37
  Erie Canal, opening of **2:**91
  Federalist Papers, The **2:**34
  first execution of a criminal by electricity **4:**51
  Hudson River **2:**94
  Hyde Park home of FDR **6:**69
  Levittowns **7:**62
  Long Island, Battle of **2:**10
  Sagamore Hill **5:**46
  Van Buren, Martin **3:**22
  West Point **2:**58
  White Plains, Battle of **2:**13
  Woodstock Festival **8:**57
New York City
  Armory Show **5:**83
  art-deco skyscrapers **6:**49
  Ashcan School **5:**80
  Bicentennial (U.S.) **8:**77
  bicycles **5:**19
  blackout of 1965 **8:**41
  Brooklyn Bridge **4:**80
  celebration of end of World War II **7:**44
  Coney Island **6:**43
  draft riots (1863) **4:**13
  Ellis Island **5:**8
  Empire State Building **6:**58
  first U.S. passenger elevator **3:**73
  General Slocum disaster **5:**52
  Holland Tunnel **6:**47
  Hudson, Henry **1:**40
  last episode of *Seinfeld* shown in Times Square **9:**95
  Lennon, John, memorial **8:**90
  Minuit, Peter **1:**48
  parade of World War I soldiers **5:**92
  Singer Building **5:**60
  Statue of Liberty **4:**88
  subways **5:**17
  temporary capital of U.S. **2:**37
  Triangle fire **5:**70
  Tweed, "Boss" **4:**54
  United Nations **7:**55
  Verrazano, Giovanni da **1:**20
  World Trade Center bombing **9:**29
New York Giants (baseball team) **7:**80, 95

New York Journal **9:**91
New York Stock Exchange **6:**55; **9:**13
New York Sun **4:**56
New York Times **6:**64; **8:**18, 49, 63
New York-to-Paris automobile race **5:**62
New York Tribune **4:**81
New York Yankees **6:**32, 86; **8:**20
Niagara (ship) **2:**72
Niagara Falls **1:**36
Nicaragua **5:**67, 74; **9:**12
Nichols, Terry **9:**42
nickelodeons **5:**50
Nicolet, Jean **1:**52
Nimitz (aircraft carrier) **7:**13
Nimitz, Chester W. **7:**51
Niña (ship) **1:**15
nitrous oxide **3:**31
Nixon, Pat **8:**54, 67
Nixon, Richard M. **7:**81; **8:**47, 53, 54, 66, 69, 73
  Cambodia, invasion of **8:**60
  Ford, Gerald R. **8:**74
  Kennedy-Nixon debates **8:**14
  oil embargo (1973) **8:**72
  resignation **4:**40
  Selective Service Act **6:**89
  space shuttles **8:**94
  Watergate scandal **8:**67
Niza, Marcos de **1:**22
Nobel Peace Prize **5:**45, 53, 54
Nobel Prize for Physics **6:**54; **7:**69
Noble, Richard **9:**83
Noonan, Fred **6:**80
Noriega, Manuel **9:**15, 18
Normandie (ship) **5:**93
Normandy (France) **7:**38
North, Oliver **9:**12, 13
North Africa, invasion of **7:**5, 9, 14, 24
North Atlantic Treaty Organization (NATO) **7:**71; **9:**51
North Carolina
  1729 **1:**68
  civil-rights sit-ins **8:**9
  Fontana Dam **6:**72
  Guilford Courthouse, Battle of **2:**27
  hurricane Hugo **9:**15
  Roanoke Island **1:**34
  tornadoes (1998) **9:**94
  White, John **1:**33
  Wright, Orville and Wilbur **5:**49
North Dakota **9:**67, 68
Northern Mariana Islands, Commonwealth of the **7:**63
Northern Pacific Railroad **4:**79
North Pole **5:**65, 66; **6:**42; **7:**94, 95
Northwest Ordinance **2:**36
Northwest Passage **1:**20, 24, 40
Northwest Territory **2:**36
Notre Dame, University of **4:**47
Nova Scotia **1:**74
nuclear fallout **8:**11
nuclear missiles **8:**21, 25
nuclear physics **6:**54
nuclear power **7:**15, 76; **8:**86
Nuclear Regulatory Commission **8:**74
nuclear submarines **7:**94, 95
"Nude Descending a Staircase" **5:**83
nullification **3:**6
Nuremberg trials **7:**57
"Nuts!" **7:**42

O

Oak Ridge (Tennessee) **7:**52
Oberlin College **3:**13
Observer (newspaper) **3:**23
ocean liners **5:**93
O'Connor, Carroll **8:**65
O'Connor, Sandra Day **8:**91
office equipment **4:**59; **5:**11
Oglethorpe, James **1:**69
O'Grady, Scott **9:**43
Ohio
  draft riots **4:**13
  Great Serpent Mound **1:**6

Hayes, Rutherford B. **4:**67
  Kent State killings **8:**59, 62
  McKinley, William **5:**23
  Northwest Territory **2:**36
  Oberlin College **3:**13
Ohio River **9:**67
oil *see* petroleum
Ojibwe (Chippewa) **1:**73
"O.K." **3:**22
O'Keeffe, Georgia **1:**41
Okinawa, Battle of **7:**51
Oklahoma **1:**10; **3:**24; **4:**94; **5:**9; **9:**42
Oklahoma! (musical) **7:**32
Oklahoma City bombing **9:**37, 42, 76
O'Laughlin, Michael **4:**33
old age *see* aging and aged
Oldenburg, Claes **8:**26
Old Faithful (geyser) **4:**55
Old Farmer's Almanac, The **2:**42
"Old Hickory" **3:**6
"Old Ironsides" *(Constitution)* (ship) **2:**46, 50, 70, 71; **9:**81
"Old Rough and Ready" **3:**56
Old South Meeting House (Boston, Massachusetts) **1:**68
Olympia (ship) **5:**30
Olympic Games
  1904 **5:**51
  1912 **5:**74
  1972 **8:**66
  1980 **8:**88
  1984 **9:**8
  1996 **9:**53, 60
  "Dream Team" **9:**26
  first modern Olympics **5:**21
  golf, early days of **5:**78
  Lipinski, Tara **9:**89
  Spitz, Mark **8:**68
  U.S. ice-hockey team (1980) **8:**89
  U.S. women gymnasts win gold (1996) **9:**61
  U.S. women win ice-hockey gold medal **9:**88
Omaha Beach **7:**38
Onassis, Jacqueline Kennedy **2:**53; **8:**32
Oñate, Juan de **1:**30
Onizuka, Ellison S. **9:**11
"Only thing we have to fear is fear itself" **6:**65
Ontario **2:**73
Operation... *see* the second part of the name
Oppenheimer, J. Robert **7:**52
Oraibi (Arizona) **1:**13
oratory *see* speeches
Oregon Territory
  1846 **3:**43
  covered wagons **3:**34
  Fort Astoria, founding of **2:**68
  Gray, Robert **2:**43
  Manifest Destiny **3:**41
  Oregon Trail **3:**33
  Polk, James K. **3:**38
Oregon Trail **3:**33
O'Reilly, Peter **3:**76
organized crime **6:**21, 56; **7:**78
Oscars *see* Academy Awards
Osceola **2:**79
O'Sullivan, John L. **3:**41
Oswald, Lee Harvey **8:**16, 28, 35
Otis, Elisha **3:**67
Ottawa Indians **1:**76
Ouimet, Francis **5:**78
Outerbridge, Mary Ewing **4:**60
outlaws **4:**74; **6:**66
Overland Mail Company **2:**85
Overlord, Operation **7:**38
Ovington, Earle **5:**72
Owen, Robert **2:**92

P

Pacific Northwest **2:**68; **3:**33
Pacific Ocean **5:**39; **6:**91; **7:**12, 37, 63
Pacific Railway Act **4:**46
Padover, Saul K. **2:**49

Pago Pago **5:**39
Pahlavi, Mohammad Reza **8:**87
painting
  Ashcan School **5:**80
  Hudson River School **2:**94
  Morse, Samuel F.B. **3:**37
  pop art **8:**26
  White, John **1:**33
Pakenham, Edward **2:**76
Palmer, A. Mitchell **6:**19
Palmetto Ranch (Texas) **4:**27
Panama **5:**51; **9:**15, 18
Panama Canal **5:**45, 54, 85, 86; **9:**18
Pan American World Airways **6:**77, 91
Panic of 1893 **5:**9
paratroopers **4:**87; **7:**33, 40, 42; **9:**6
Paris, liberation of **7:**39
Paris, Treaty of **2:**29
Parker, Alton B. **5:**51
Parker, Bonnie **6:**66
Parker, Charlie **6:**29
Parks, Rosa **7:**89, 90
Parrott, Jacob **4:**7
party lines **4:**65
Pasteur, Louis **3:**69
Patent Office, U.S. **2:**74
Pathfinder mission to Mars **9:**79
Patterson, John H. **4:**69
Patton, George **5:**90; **7:**24, 25, 48
"Paul Revere's Ride" **1:**89
Pawnee Indians **2:**81
Pawtucket (Rhode Island) **2:**39
Paxton Boys **1:**77
Payne, Lewis **4:**33
Peabody Award **9:**36
Peace Corps **8:**16, 17
Peace Democrats **4:**18
Pearl Harbor, attack on **2:**46; **6:**90, 96
Peary, Robert E. **5:**65, 66
Pemberton, John **4:**90
Pendleton Civil Service Act **4:**73
Peninsular Campaign **3:**88
Penn, William **1:**58, 61
Pennsylvania
  1682 **1:**58
  1692 **1:**61
  first oil well **3:**75
  Gettysburg, Battle of **4:**10
  Gettysburg National Military Park **4:**11
  Homestead Strike **5:**6
  Johnstown flood **4:**93
  Paxton Boys **1:**77
  steel industry **5:**40
  Three Mile Island accident **8:**86
  Valley Forge National Historical Park **2:**20
  Whiskey Rebellion **2:**47
  see also Philadelphia
Pennsylvania Gazette **1:**68
pensions **6:**75
Pentagon Papers **8:**63
Perils of Pauline, The **5:**79
Perkins, Frances **6:**67
Perot, Ross **9:**23, 53, 66
Perry, Matthew C. **2:**72; **3:**58, 65
Perry, Oliver Hazard **2:**72, 73; **3:**65
Perryville, Battle of **3:**94
Pershing, John J. **5:**90; **6:**13
Persian Gulf War **9:**21, 22
  aircraft carriers **7:**13
  Bush, George **9:**16
  integrated armed forces **9:**87
  Powell, Colin **9:**46
  Strategic Air Command **7:**58
personal computers **8:**83
Personal Responsibility and Work Opportunity Reconciliation Act **9:**63
Petersburg, Siege of **4:**22
petroleum (oil)
  Exxon Valdez oil spill **9:**15, 17
  first oil well **3:**73, 75
  oil embargo (1973) **8:**69, 72
  Persian Gulf War **9:**21

petroleum (oil) (cont.)
plastics **4**:43
Spindletop **5**:44
Teapot Dome scandal **6**:34
Texas **5**:43
Trans-Alaska Pipeline **8**:82
Phantom Empire **5**:79
Phelps, Jaycie **9**:61
Phi Beta Kappa **1**:63
Philadelphia (Pennsylvania)
Bicentennial (U.S.) **8**:77
Centennial Exposition (1876) **4**:62, 64
Constitutional Convention **2**:33
department stores **4**:44
first U.S. medical school **1**:81
Independence National Historical Park **2**:9
Liberty Bell **2**:8
Presidents' Summit for America's Future **9**:75
Philadelphia Athletics **4**:54
Philip (prince of Great Britain) **7**:92
Philip, King *see* Metacomet
Philip II (king of Spain) **1**:31
Philippines
1898 **5**:27
1944 **7**:33
Bataan **7**:6
Leyte Gulf, Battle of **7**:41
Manifest Destiny **3**:41
Manila Bay, Battle of **5**:30
Spanish-American War **5**:28; **9**:91
Taft, William Howard **5**:63
U.S. takeover **5**:31
phonograph **4**:68
photocopiers **6**:84
photography **4**:91; **7**:64
physics **6**:54; **7**:15; **8**:13
Picasso, Pablo **5**:83
Pickett, George E. **4**:10
Pickett's Charge **4**:5
Pickford, Mary **6**:6
Pierce, Charlotte Woodward **3**:52
Pierce, Franklin **3**:62, 63, 64
Pike, Zebulon **2**:64; **6**:53
Pikes Peak **2**:64; **4**:49
Pilgrims
1620 **1**:44
Mayflower Compact **1**:45
Plimoth Plantation **1**:46
Puritans compared to **1**:49
Thanksgiving **1**:47
pillory **1**:57
Pinkerton, Allan **3**:82
Pinkertons **5**:6
Pinta (ship) **1**:15
pioneer life
covered wagons **3**:34
Donner party **3**:47
log cabins **1**:51
Oregon Trail **3**:33
sod houses **4**:35
Winchester rifle **4**:50
pipelines **8**:72, 82
Piper, Lon **6**:53
Pippen, Scottie **9**:26
pirates and piracy **1**:66; **2**:57
Pitcairn, John **1**:90
Pitcher, Molly **2**:21
Pizarro, Francisco **1**:27
Plains Indians **1**:11
plantations **2**:60
plastics **4**:43
Pledge of Allegiance **5**:7
Plessy, Homer **5**:22
Plessy v. *Ferguson* **5**:22
Plimoth Plantation **1**:46
plow, steel **3**:26
plutonium **9**:84
Plymouth (Massachusetts) **1**:44, 46, 47
Plymouth Rock **1**:44
Pocahontas **1**:37, 38
poetry **1**:89; **2**:50
Poitier, Sidney **6**:74
Poland **9**:19
Polaroid camera **7**:64

police **4**:86; **8**:42; **9**:35
police brutality **8**:37; **9**:24
polio **6**:65, 68; **7**:49, 83
Polk, James K. **3**:35, 38, 43
pollution *see* environment
Polynesia **5**:39
Ponce de León, Juan **1**:19; **5**:37
ponies *see* horses
Pontiac's Rebellion **1**:76
Pony Express **3**:77, 78
Poor Richard's Almanack **2**:42
pop art **8**:26
Pope, John **3**:90
Porgy and Bess (opera) **6**:74
Port Moresby (New Guinea) **7**:11
Portsmouth, Treaty of **5**:53
Portsmouth (New Hampshire) draft riots **4**:13
Post, Charles **5**:42
Post, Marjorie Merriweather **6**:27
postal services **1**:61, 88; **2**:85; **3**:77; **5**:72; **6**:5
poster for Liberty bonds **6**:6
Potomac River **3**:74
Potsdam Conference **7**:53
pottery **1**:23
poverty **4**:95; **8**:40; **9**:63
Poverty, War on **8**:32
Poverty Point (Louisiana) **1**:5
Powell, Colin **9**:46, 75, 87
Powell, John Wesley **4**:53
Powers, Francis Gary **8**:12
Powhatan **1**:37
Powhatan Indians **1**:38
powwows **1**:73
prayer in public schools **8**:21
prejudice and discrimination
arson destruction of African-American churches **9**:52
Ku Klux Klan **4**:41
Scottsboro case **6**:60
Prendergast, Maurice **5**:83
Presbyterians **1**:67
Prescott, William **1**:92
presidents of the U.S.
former generals **9**:46
22nd Constitutional Amendment **7**:76
White House **2**:53
see also elections, presidential; names of presidents
Presidents' Summit for America's Future **9**:75
Presley, Elvis **7**:90, 95
press, freedom of the **1**:71; **2**:51; **3**:23; **8**:63
Preston, Thomas **1**:84
Pretty Woman **9**:19
Préval, René **9**:35
Price Administration, Office of **7**:16
Princeton, Battle of **2**:16, 17
Princeton University **1**:67; **5**:81
Princeton, U.S.S. (ship) **3**:35
Prince William Sound **9**:15, 17
printing **4**:81
prisoners of war
Allies cross the Rhine **7**:48
Andersonville Prison **4**:19
Pueblo incident **8**:49
Procter, Henry **2**:73
Profiles in Courage **8**:16
Progressive Party (Bull Moose Party) **5**:45, 63, 74, 76
Prohibition era **6**:21, 22, 32, 56, 67, 71
Project Independence **8**:72
Promise Keepers rally **9**:82
Promontory (Utah) **4**:46
Prophet, The *see* Tenskwatawa
Protestantism **1**:49, 53, 67
public education **5**:12; **8**:21
public libraries **4**:52
publishing **2**:42, 54
see also newspapers
Pueblo Bonito **1**:7
Pueblo incident **8**:49
Pueblo Indians **1**:23, 41
Puerto Rico **1**:19; **5**:27, 28, 32, 37; **9**:91

Pulitzer Prizes **7**:72; **8**:16
Pullman, George **4**:36; **5**:94
Pullman car **4**:36; **5**:94
Pullman strike **5**:16
puppets **8**:58
Pure Food and Drug Act **5**:54, 56
Puritans **1**:49, 53
Purity Distilling Company **6**:20
Pyle, Ernie **7**:28

Q

Quakers **1**:61
Quayle, Dan **9**:23
Quebec **1**:24, 36, 72, 88
Quebec City (Quebec) **1**:24, 94
Queen Elizabeth (ship) **5**:93
Queensberry rules **4**:76
Quintanilla Perez, Selena *see* Selena
quiz show scandal **8**:6

R

race
Japanese-Americans, internment of **7**:5, 20
Ku Klux Klan's racism **4**:41
Show Boat **6**:48
see also African-Americans; desegregation
radio
big bands **6**:76
Coolidge was first president to address nation on radio **6**:32
De Forest, Lee **5**:69
early radio **6**:62
first radio broadcast **6**:62
FM radio **6**:62
Harding's victory broadcast **6**:21
Roosevelt's "fireside chats" **6**:68
Scopes trial **6**:40
Radio City Music Hall **6**:49
railroads
1829 **3**:5
1893 **5**:9
1950 **7**:73
buffalo, decline of **4**:42
cog railways **4**:49
Cooper's *Tom Thumb* **3**:9
Credit Mobilier scandal **4**:56
Gadsden Purchase **3**:64
Long, Stephen H. **2**:81
luxury travel **5**:94
Pullman's sleeping car **4**:36
Pullman strike **5**:16
strike (1884) **4**:84
subways **5**:17
transcontinental railroad **4**:46, 79
Westinghouse's air brake **4**:51
Rainier (prince of Monaco) **7**:90
Rains, Claude **7**:19
Raleigh, Sir Walter **1**:33
rallies
"Million Man March" **9**:50
Promise Keepers **9**:82
"Stand for Children" **9**:57
see also demonstrations and protests
Ramirez, Patricia **9**:57
ranching **4**:58
rape (Scottsboro case) **6**:60
Rather, Dan **8**:51
rationing **6**:90; **7**:5, 16, 21, 33
Ray, James Earl **8**:50
Raytheon Laboratories **8**:46
razors **5**:20
Reagan, Nancy **9**:75
Reagan, Ronald **8**:88, 91, 92; **9**:8, 13
assassination attempt **8**:93
bomb attack on U.S. Marines in Lebanon **9**:5
Casablanca **7**:19
Ford, Gerald R. **8**:74
Grenada, invasion of **9**:6
Iran-contra affair **9**:12
Reasoner, Harry **8**:51

rebellions and uprisings
Bacon's Rebellion **1**:56
Pontiac's Rebellion **1**:76
Shays' Rebellion **2**:31
Turner's rebellion **3**:11
Whiskey Rebellion **2**:47
Reconstruction period **4**:40, 41
recordings, sound **4**:68; **9**:7
Red Cross, founding of the **4**:75
Redford, Robert **6**:39
Red River of the North **9**:67
Red Scare of 1919–1920 **6**:19
Reed, Walter **5**:34
Reese, Pee Wee **7**:60
refrigerators **5**:84
Rehnquist, William H. **9**:69
Reiner, Rob **8**:65
religion *see* names of religions
religion, freedom of **1**:44, 78; **8**:21
Remagen (Germany) **7**:48
"Remember the Alamo!" **3**:17, 18
"Remember the *Maine*!" **5**:29
Remington typewriter **4**:59
Republican Party
1994 **9**:34
Congress, control of **9**:37, 38, 66
election of 1912 **5**:76
founding of **3**:66
Manifest Destiny **3**:41
presidential primaries (1996) **9**:54
Resaca de la Palma, Battle of **3**:43
rescue of Scott O'Grady **9**:43
reservations, Indian **2**:89
Resnik, Judith A. **9**:11
respirators **5**:38
Restore Hope, Operation **9**:27
retailing
cash registers **4**:69
department stores **4**:44
rationing **7**:16
Woolworth's store closings **9**:80
Yankee peddlers **2**:44
Retton, Mary Lou **9**:8
Return of the Jedi, The **8**:84
Revenue Marine **2**:40
Revere, Paul **1**:84, 88, 89, 91
revival meetings **1**:67
Revolutionary War **1**:88; **2**:5, 16, 21, 25
Adams, John **2**:49
Articles of Confederation **2**:19
Boston Massacre **1**:84
Boston Tea Party **1**:85, 86
Bunker Hill, Battle of **1**:92
Bushnell's submarine *Turtle* **2**:12
cannon of Ticonderoga **2**:6
Continental Congress, First **1**:87
Cowpens, Battle of **2**:26
Declaration of Independence **2**:7
Green Mountain Boys **1**:96
Guilford Courthouse, Battle of **2**:27
Hale, Nathan **2**:11
Jackson, Andrew **3**:6
King's Mountain, Battle of **2**:24
Long Island, Battle of **2**:10
Minute Man National Historical Park **1**:91
Minutemen **1**:90
Monmouth, Battle of **2**:23
Monroe, James **2**:78
Monticello **1**:83
Paris, Treaty of **2**:29
Princeton, Battle of **2**:17
Quebec City, invasion of **1**:94
Revere, Paul **1**:89
Saratoga campaign **2**:18
Second Continental Congress **1**:93
Trenton, Battle of **2**:15
Valley Forge **2**:20
Washington, George **2**:38
Washington crosses the Delaware **2**:14

White Plains, Battle of **2:**13
Yorktown, British surrender at **2:**28
revolvers **3:**20
revues **5:**59
Rhine River **7:**40, 48
Rhode Island **1:**78; **2:**33, 39
Rhodes, James **8:**62
Ribaut, Jean **1:**29
Rice, Dan **2:**77
Richards, Michael **9:**95
Richmond (Virginia) **2:**25; **3:**88; **4:**22, 28
Rickenbacker, Eddie **7:**61
Rickey, Branch **7:**60
rifles **4:**50
Riis, Jacob **4:**95
Riley, Fort **6:**16
riots
    antitax riots (1765) **1:**81
    Bonus Army **6:**61
    Detroit (1967) **8:**44
    draft riots (1863) **4:**13
    Haymarket Riot (1886) **4:**86
    King assassination aftermath **8:**50
    Los Angeles (1992) **9:**23, 24
    Springfield, Illinois (1908) **5:**64
Ripken, Cal, Jr. **6:**86
"Rip Van Winkle" **2:**80
Ritty, James **4:**69
rivers **2:**65; **9:**55
Rivers, Ruben **9:**70
roads and highways **2:**59; **3:**40; **8:**72
Roanoke Island **1:**33, 34
Roaring Twenties **6:**30
Roberts, Montague **5:**62
Roberts, Needham **6:**7
Robinson, David **9:**26
Robinson, Jackie **7:**60
Rockefeller, John D. (1839–1937) **5:**71, 87
Rockefeller, John D., Jr. **1:**50
Rockefeller family **1:**63; **7:**55
rockets and missiles **6:**41; **7:**58; **8:**25; **9:**64
rock music **7:**90, 95; **8:**33, 57
Rockwell, Norman **5:**68; **7:**17
Rocky Mountain Fur Company **2:**86
Rocky Mountains **2:**64
Rodgers, Calbraith **5:**71
Rodgers, Richard **7:**32
Roebling, John and Washington **4:**80
Roe v. *Wade* **8:**69
Rogers, Will **5:**59
Rolfe, John **1:**37
Roman Catholics in America **1:**70, 82; **8:**16; **9:**49
Rommel, Erwin **7:**24
Rooney, Andy **8:**51
Roosevelt, Eleanor **6:**69, 85; **7:**49
Roosevelt, Franklin Delano **6:**68, 73, 79, 85, 90; **7:**33, 44
    Atlantic Charter **6:**92
    death **7:**49
    early radio **6:**35
    election of 1932 **6:**65
    Empire State Building **6:**58
    G.I. Bill **7:**43
    Hyde Park home **6:**69
    New Deal political cartoon **6:**67
    Pearl Harbor **6:**96
    Selective Service Act **6:**89
    Supreme Court **6:**83
    third term **6:**88
    Yalta Conference **7:**46
    see also New Deal
Roosevelt, Sara **6:**69
Roosevelt, Theodore **5:**27, 43, 45, 51, 54, 74
    election of 1912 **5:**76
    football, early days of **4:**47
    Great White Fleet **5:**58
    Mount Rushmore **6:**93
    Nobel Peace Prize **5:**53
    Panama **9:**18
    Panama Canal **5:**86
    Rough Riders **5:**33
    Sagamore Hill **5:**46

Taft, William Howard **5:**63
White House **2:**53
Roots **8:**81
Rosalie (mansion) **3:**40
Rosalie, Fort **1:**68; **3:**40
Rose, Pete **6:**18
Rosecrans, William S. **3:**96; **4:**14
Rosenberg, Julius and Ethel **7:**85
Rosie the Riveter **7:**17
Ross, Betsy **8:**15
Ross, Robert **2:**74
Roswell Incident **9:**78
Rota **7:**63
Roughing It **3:**76
Rough Riders **5:**27, 33
Rowlandson, Mary **1:**58
Royal Gorge Bridge **6:**53
rubber, vulcanized **3:**27
"Rubber Duckie" (song) **8:**58
Ruby, Jack **8:**28, 35
rum **1:**64
Rushmore, Mount **6:**93
Rusk, Dean **8:**25
Russell, Lillian **5:**19
Russia **4:**38; **5:**53; **6:**11; **9:**44
    see also Union of Soviet Socialist Republics
Russo-Japanese War **5:**53
Ruth, Babe **6:**44, 86
Rutland (Vermont) draft riots **4:**13

S

Sabin, Albert **7:**83
Sacagawea **2:**62
Sacco-Vanzetti case **6:**23
Sadat, Anwar **8:**85
Safer, Morley **8:**51
safety, workplace **5:**70
Sagamore Hill **5:**46
Saigon (Vietnam) **8:**70
St. Augustine (Florida) **1:**31
St. Croix **5:**96
St. Helens, Mount **8:**88
St. John **5:**96
St. Lawrence River **1:**24
St. Lawrence Seaway **8:**5
St. Louis (Missouri) **1:**51
St. Mihiel, Battle of **6:**13
St. Paul (Minnesota) **3:**48
"Saints" *see* Pilgrims
St. Thomas **5:**96
St. Valentine's Day Massacre **6:**56
Saipan **7:**37, 63
Saldivar, Yolanda **9:**41
Salem witch-hunt **1:**61, 62
Salk, Jonas **7:**83
Salvation Army **4:**70
Samoa, American **5:**39
San Antonio (Texas) **1:**66, 70; **3:**17
San Antonio Missions National Historical Park **1:**70
Sandford, John **3:**70
San Diego (California) **1:**28
Sandwich Islands **2:**22
San Francisco (California)
    earthquake (1906) **5:**54, 55
    Golden Gate Bridge **6:**81
San Francisco Giants baseball **7:**80
San Ildefonso pueblo **1:**23
San Jacinto, Battle of **3:**16, 17, 18, 49, 50
San Juan (Puerto Rico) **5:**37
San Juan Capistrano (California) **1:**82
San Salvador **1:**15
Santa Anna, Antonio López de **3:**17, 18, 49, 50
Santa Barbara (California) **1:**82
Santa Clara pueblo **1:**23
Santa Fe (New Mexico) **2:**83
Santa Fe Trail **2:**83
Santa Maria (ship) **1:**15
Saratoga campaign **1:**94; **2:**16, 18
satellites, artificial
    Skylab **8:**71
    Sputnik I **7:**92
    Telstar I **8:**23
    weather satellites **8:**10
Saturday Night Fever **8:**79

Saturn space probe **9:**84
Saudi Arabia **9:**58
Saunders, Joe W. **1:**5
Savannah (Georgia) **4:**18, 26
Savannah (ship) **2:**80
Sawyer, Diane **8:**51
Sawyer, Tom **4:**83
scandals *see* ethics and corruption
Scheuer, Sandra **8:**62
Schmidt, Harry **7:**47
schools *see* colleges and universities; education
Schroeder, William **8:**62
Schuster, George **5:**62
Schwarzkopf, H. Norman **9:**22
Schwerner, Michael **8:**34
science
    Skylab **8:**71
    Wilkes expedition **3:**25
    see also astronomy; physics
science fiction
    E.T., the Extra-Terrestrial **8:**95
    Star Trek **8:**43
    Star Wars trilogy **8:**84
    3-D movies **7:**82
Scobee, Francis R. **9:**11
Scopes, John **6:**40
Scopes trial **6:**40
Scott, Dave **8:**64
Scott, Dred **3:**70
Scott, Winfield **3:**48, 50
Scottsboro case **6:**60
scouting *see* Boy Scouts; Girl Scouts
sculpture
    Iwo Jima memorial **7:**47
    Mount Rushmore **6:**93
    Statue of Liberty **4:**88
    Vietnam Veterans Memorial **8:**96
seaplanes **5:**73
Seattle (Washington) **4:**85; **5:**26
Seattle Metropolitans **5:**48
secession of Confederate states **3:**78, 79; **4:**32, 39
Second Continental Congress *see* Continental Congress, Second
Secret Service **4:**72
Securities and Exchange Commission **6:**55
Sedition Act *see* Alien and Sedition Acts
segregation
    Montgomery bus boycott **7:**89, 90
    Plessy v. *Ferguson* **5:**22
    sit-ins **8:**9
    see also desegregation
Seinfeld **9:**95
Seinfeld, Jerry **9:**95
Selective Service Act **6:**89
Selena **9:**41
Selma (Alabama) **8:**37
Selma-to-Montgomery marches **8:**37
Selznick, David O. **6:**87
Seminoles **2:**79
Seminole Wars **2:**79, 82; **3:**56
Semmes, Raphael **4:**23
Senate, U.S.
    1994 **9:**34
    Adams, John Quincy **2:**90
    Army-McCarthy hearings **7:**86
    Buchanan, James **3:**71
    Davis, Jefferson **3:**83
    Harrison, Benjamin **4:**92
    Harrison, William Henry **3:**29
    Johnson, Andrew **4:**32, 40
    Johnson, Lyndon Baines **8:**32
    Kefauver Crime Commission **7:**78
    Kennedy, John F. **8:**16
    Kennedy, Robert F. **8:**52
    Monroe, James **2:**78
    Van Buren, Martin **3:**22
Seneca Falls Convention **3:**52, 53; **6:**24
Senegal **9:**92
senior citizens *see* aging and aged
Sennett, Mack **5:**50

septuplets **9:**85
Sequoia National Park **4:**95
Sergeant York **6:**14
Serra, Junípero **1:**82
Servicemen's Readjustment Act *see* G.I. Bill
Sesame Street **8:**58
Seven Days, Battle of the **3:**88
Seward, William H. **4:**30, 33, 38
sewing machines **3:**44
Shadow, The **6:**35
Shakers **3:**46
Shapiro, Robert **9:**40
Shaw, Robert Gould **4:**12
Shawnees **2:**69
Shays' Rebellion **2:**31
sheep, cloning of **9:**68, 73
Shenandoah River **3:**74
Shenandoah Valley campaign **4:**25
Shepard, Alan B., Jr. **8:**19
Sheridan, Philip **4:**25
Sherman, William Tecumseh **4:**18, 24, 26; **7:**8
Sherman Antitrust Act **4:**95; **5:**71
Sherman's March to the Sea **4:**26
Sherman tanks **7:**8
Shiloh, Battle of **3:**86, 89; **4:**53
Shinn, Everett **5:**80
ships and shipping
    aircraft carriers **7:**13
    Andrea Doria **7:**91
    Arthur's modernization of Navy **4:**73
    clipper ships **3:**51
    Coast Guard, U.S. **2:**40
    Exxon Valdez oil spill **9:**15, 17
    Great White Fleet **5:**58
    Inchon, landing at **7:**75
    Lusitania **5:**89
    Maine, USS **5:**29
    Mayflower **1:**44
    Monitor vs. the *Merrimack* **3:**87
    Nautilus **7:**94
    Navy, United States **2:**46
    ocean liners **5:**93
    "Old Ironsides" **2:**50; **9:**81
    Panama Canal **5:**86
    Pearl Harbor attack **6:**96
    St. Lawrence Seaway **8:**5
    slave trade **2:**65
    steam power **2:**80
    Titanic **5:**75
    see also submarines
Shockley, William **7:**69
Sholes, Christopher Latham **4:**59
"shot heard round the world" **1:**90
Shoup, David M. **7:**31
Show Boat (musical) **5:**59; **6:**48
Shughart, Randall D. **4:**7
Sicily, invasion of **7:**25
sideburns **3:**95
Signal Corps, U.S. **5:**72
silent movies **5:**50
silver **1:**89; **3:**73, 76
Simpson, Nicole Brown **9:**34, 40, 65
Simpson, O.J. **9:**34, 37, 40, 65
Sinagua Indians **1:**8
Sinai Peninsula **8:**85
Sinatra, Frank **6:**76
Sinclair, Madge **8:**81
Sinclair, Upton **5:**56
Singer, I.M. **3:**44
Singer Building **5:**60
Sioux Indians **4:**63, 96
sit-ins **8:**9
$64,000 Question **8:**6
60 Minutes **8:**51
Skagway (Alaska) **5:**26
Sketch Book **2:**80
Skylab **8:**71
skyscrapers **5:**60; **6:**49, 58
Slater, Samuel **2:**39
slavery **1:**42; **3:**16, 57; **4:**5
    Amistad case **3:**28
    "Bleeding Kansas" **3:**68
    boxing, early days of **4:**76
    Buchanan, James **3:**71
    Compromise of 1850 **3:**58
    cotton gin **2:**48

slavery (cont.)
cotton-textile industry **2**:39
Dred Scott decision **3**:70
Emancipation Proclamation **4**:6
end of slave trade **2**:65
first captive Africans brought to
Virginia **1**:43
Fugitive Slave Act **3**:59
Lincoln-Douglas debates **3**:72
Northwest Ordinance forbade
2:36
plantations **2**:60
Republican Party, founding of
3:66
Roots **8**:81
triangular slave trade **1**:64
Turner's rebellion **3**:11
Underground Railroad **3**:21
Vermont first state to abolish
2:16
Vesey, Denmark **2**:84
Washington, George **1**:75
see also abolition
Sloan, John **5**:80, 83
Smith, Jedediah **2**:87
Smith, John **1**:37, 38
Smith, Joseph **3**:36
Smith, Michael J. **9**:11
Smithson, James **3**:45
Smithsonian Institution **3**:45; **4**:53;
5:25
smuggling **2**:40
Snake Dance **1**:6, 13
Social Security Act **6**:68, 73, 75
social welfare **9**:63
sod houses **4**:34, 35
Sojourner (robot rover) **9**:68, 79
solar cells **8**:10
Solomon Islands, Battle of the **7**:29,
30
Somalia, American troops in **9**:27
Sons of Liberty **1**:79, 80; **2**:5
sound barrier, breaking of **9**:83
South, the **2**:60; **4**:39; **9**:94
see also Confederate States of
America
South Africa **9**:19
South Carolina
1729 **1**:68
Cowpens, Battle of **2**:26
Fort Sumter National Monument
3:84
Fort Wagner, Battle of **4**:12
hurricane Hugo **9**:15
King's Mountain, Battle of **2**:24
Ribaut, Jean **1**:29
secession **3**:78, 79
tornadoes (1998) **9**:94
Vesey, Denmark **2**:84
South Dakota **4**:96; **6**:93; **9**:67, 68
Southern Pacific Railroad **3**:64
South Pass **2**:87
South Pole **6**:42
Southwest
Coronado, Francisco Vásquez
de **1**:25
Dust Bowl **6**:57
Manifest Destiny **3**:41
Powell, John Wesley **4**:53
Pueblo Indians **1**:23
Santa Fe Trail **2**:83
*Sovereignty and Goodness of God,
The* **1**:58
Soviet Union *see* Union of Soviet
Socialist Republics
Soyuz (spacecraft) **8**:76
space exploration and travel **7**:95;
8:21, 28, 47
Apollo 1 tragedy **8**:39, 44, 45
Apollo-Soyuz Test Project **8**:76
Cassini space probe **9**:84
Challenger disaster **9**:11
docking of *Atlantis* and *Mir* **9**:44
Gemini missions **8**:36
Goddard, Robert **6**:41
Hubble Space Telescope **9**:20,
62
moon landing **8**:55
Pathfinder mission to Mars **9**:79

Shepard, Alan, first American in
space **8**:19
Skylab **8**:71
space shuttles **8**:94
Telstar I **8**:23
Viking Mars probes **8**:77, 78
weather satellites **8**:10
White, Ed, "walks" in space
8:39
space shuttles **8**:91, 94
Challenger disaster **9**:11
Discovery and Hubble Space
Telescope **9**:20
docking of *Atlantis* and *Mir* **9**:44
Endeavour and Hubble Space
Telescope **9**:20
space stations **8**:71; **9**:44
Spain
1541 **1**:26
California missions **1**:82
Florida ceded to U.S. **2**:82
Maine, USS, sinking of the **5**:29
St. Augustine **1**:31
Spanish-American War **5**:28;
9:91
Spangler, Ned **4**:33
Spanish-American War **5**:27, 28
Guam **5**:36
Maine, USS, sinking of the **5**:29
Manila Bay, Battle of **5**:30
McKinley, William **5**:23
100th anniversary **9**:91
overseas possessions **5**:43
Philippines, U.S. takeover of
5:31
Puerto Rico **5**:32, 37
Reed, Walter **5**:34
Rough Riders **5**:33
Wake Island **6**:91
Spanish in America
Cabrillo, Juan Rodríguez **1**:28
Oñate, Juan de **1**:30
San Antonio Missions National
Historical Park **1**:70
Taos **1**:41
speakeasies **6**:21, 22
speech, freedom of **2**:51; **5**:7
speeches
"Checkers" speech (Nixon) **7**:81
Clinton, Hillary, in China **9**:47
Gettysburg Address **3**:81; **4**:16;
6:31
Hale, Nathan **2**:11
Henry, Patrick **1**:79, 81
"I have a dream" (King) **6**:31;
8:31
Kennedy's speech in Berlin **8**:29
speed skating **8**:89
Spencer, Percy **8**:46
Spielberg, Steven **8**:95
spies *see* espionage
Spindletop **5**:44
Spirit of St. Louis (airplane) **6**:46
Spitz, Mark **8**:66, 68
spoils system **3**:5
sports *see* Olympic Games; names
of sports
Spotsylvania, Battle of **4**:21
Springfield (Massachusetts) **5**:5
Springfield (Illinois) race riots **5**:64
Springwood (Hyde Park, New York)
6:69
Sputnik (space capsule) **7**:92; **8**:19,
76
Stafford, Tom **8**:76
stagecoaches **2**:85; **3**:55
Stahl, Lesley **8**:51
Stalin, Joseph **7**:46, 53
Stamp Act **1**:79, 80, 81
stamps, postage **3**:64; **5**:72
Standard Oil Company of Ohio **5**:71
"Stand for Children" **9**:57
Standish, Miles **1**:45
Stanky, Eddie **7**:60
Stanley, Francis and Freelan **5**:24
Stanley Cup **5**:48
Stanley Steamer **5**:24
Stanton, Edwin M. **4**:39
Stanton, Elizabeth Cady **3**:52; **6**:24

Stapleton, Jean **8**:65
Stark, John **2**:16
Starr, Bart **8**:44
Starr, Kenneth W. **9**:96
Starr, Ringo **8**:33
"Star-Spangled Banner, The" **2**:71;
8:57
Star Trek **8**:43
starving time (of Jamestown) **1**:37
Star Wars (movie) **8**:84
State, U.S. Dept. of **3**:22, 71; **9**:71
states' rights **2**:80; **3**:30
Statue of Liberty **4**:85, 88; **8**:77
statues *see* sculpture
stealth bombers **9**:33
steam power **2**:65, 80, 93; **3**:9; **5**:24
steel industry **5**:6, 40; **7**:81
Steinbeck, John **6**:57
Stempel, Herbert **8**:6
Stevenson, Adlai (1900–1965) **7**:81
Stewart, Lazarus **1**:77
Stimson, Henry **6**:89
Stockholm (ship) **7**:91
stock market **5**:9; **6**:50, 55; **9**:13
stocks (punishment) **1**:57
Stockton, John **9**:26
stomp grounds of Cherokees **1**:10
Stones River, Battle of *see*
Murfreesboro, Battle of
Stones River National Battlefield
3:96
Stowe, Harriet Beecher **3**:62
"Strangers" *see* Pilgrims
Strategic Air Command **7**:58
Strauss, Joseph B. **6**:81
strikes
1886 **4**:85
1950 **7**:73
1952 **7**:81
baseball (1994) **9**:34
Homestead Strike **5**:6
Lowell "mill girls" **3**:19
Ludlow Massacre **5**:85, 87
Pullman strike **5**:16
railroads (1884) **4**:84
Stringfield, Sherry **9**:36
Strom, Robert **8**:6
Strug, Kerri **9**:53, 61
Struthers, Sally **8**:65
Stuart, Gilbert **2**:38
student protests (1970) **8**:59
Studio 54 (nightclub) **8**:79
submarines **2**:12; **5**:38; **7**:94
subways **5**:17
Suez crisis **7**:90
suffrage **8**:37
see also woman suffrage
sugar **1**:64; **7**:16
Sullivan, John L. **4**:76
Sullivan, "Smiling Jim" **7**:78
Summer, Donna **8**:79
Sumter, Fort **3**:79, 80, 84
Sumter, Thomas **3**:84
Sundback, Gideon **5**:14
Sunset Crater **1**:8
Super Bowl **8**:44
Supreme Court
1803 **2**:61
Amistad case **3**:28
Brown v. Board of Education
7:87
Dred Scott decision **3**:70
income tax **5**:82; **6**:44
McCulloch v. Maryland **2**:80
Miranda decision **8**:42
Montgomery bus boycott **7**:89
O'Connor, Sandra Day **8**:91
Pentagon Papers **8**:63
Pledge of Allegiance **5**:7
Plessy v. Ferguson **5**:22
prayer in public schools **8**:21
Roosevelt, Franklin D. **6**:83
Scottsboro case **6**:60
Standard Oil Company **5**:71
Taft, William Howard **5**:63
surgery **3**:31; **5**:9
Suribachi, Mount **7**:47
Surratt, Mary **4**:33
Susan Constant (ship) **1**:37, 39

Sutter, John **3**:54, 55
swallows of San Juan Capistrano
1:82
Swanson Foods **7**:70
sweatshops **5**:70
swimming **8**:68
swing music **6**:29, 76
Symbionese Liberation Army **8**:75
synagogues **1**:78

T

Taft, William Howard **1**:65; **5**:60, 63,
67, 74, 76
Tallapoosa River **2**:75
tanks, Sherman **7**:8
Taos (New Mexico) **1**:41
Tarawa **7**:31
Tarleton, Banastre **2**:26
Tate, Sharon **8**:56
taxation
1765 **1**:81
Bacon's Rebellion **1**:56
Boston Tea Party **1**:85, 86
Capone, Al, evasion **6**:56
Forbes, Steve, in 1996
Republican primaries **9**:54
French and Indian War **1**:72
income tax **5**:82; **6**:44; **7**:21
Social Security Act **6**:75
Stamp Act **1**:80
Whiskey Rebellion **2**:47
Taylor, Zachary **3**:43, 49, 53, 55, 56,
57
tea **1**:85, 86; **5**:51
Tea Act **1**:85
Teach, Edward *see* Blackbeard
Teapot Dome scandal **6**:25, 34
Tecumseh **2**:69, 73; **4**:26
teddy bears **5**:45
Tejano music **9**:41
telegraph **3**:35, 37, 77, 80
telephone **4**:64, 65; **5**:9; **8**:13, 23
telescopes **9**:20, 32, 62
television
1939 **6**:85
1951 **7**:76
All in the Family **8**:65
Army-McCarthy hearings **7**:86
Cosby Show, The **9**:10
Disney–ABC merger **9**:45
ER **9**:36
I Love Lucy **7**:79
Kefauver Crime Commission
7:78
Kennedy-Nixon debates **8**:14
Miss America Pageant **6**:26
popularity increases **7**:70
quiz show scandal **8**:6
Roots **8**:81
Seinfeld **9**:95
Sesame Street **8**:58
60 Minutes **8**:51
Star Trek **8**:43
Telstar I **8**:23
Telstar I **8**:23
Tennessee
Chattanooga, Battle of **4**:15
Hermitage, the **3**:14
Johnson, Andrew **4**:32
Mississippi River flood (1927)
6:45
Murfreesboro, Battle of **3**:96
Natchez Trace National
Parkway **2**:59
Scopes trial **6**:40
Shiloh, Battle of **3**:89
tornadoes (1998) **9**:94
Tennessee River **6**:72; **9**:67
Tennessee Valley Authority **6**:72
Tennet, Gilbert **1**:67
tennis, early days of **4**:60
Tenskwatawa **2**:69
Teresa, Mother, death of **9**:68
territorial expansion
1847 **3**:48
1898 **5**:27
Alaska **4**:38
Florida **2**:82
Gadsden Purchase **3**:64

Guam **5**:36
Hawaii **5**:35
Lewis and Clark expedition **2**:62
Louisiana Purchase **2**:61
Manifest Destiny **3**:41
Northwest Ordinance **2**:36
Philippines **5**:31
Polk, James K. **3**:38
Puerto Rico, takeover of **5**:32
Spanish-American War **5**:43
Virgin Islands, U.S. **5**:96
terrorism
  Ku Klux Klan **4**:41
  Oklahoma City bombing **9**:37, 42, 76
  Saudi Arabian bombing of U.S. troops **9**:58
  Unabomber arrest **9**:56
  World Trade Center bombing **9**:29
Tesla, Nikola **4**:51
Tet Offensive **8**:47
Texas
  1836 **3**:16
  1846 **3**:43
  Alamo, Battle of the **3**:17
  annexation **3**:35
  cowboys and cattle drives **4**:37
  Johnson, Lyndon Baines **8**:32
  Manifest Destiny **3**:41
  oil strike **5**:43
  San Antonio Missions National Historical Park **1**:70
  San Jacinto, Battle of **3**:18
  Selena, murder of **9**:41
  Spindletop **5**:44
  Tyler, John **3**:30
  Van Buren, Martin **3**:22
  Waco raid **9**:30
textile industry **2**:39; **3**:19
Thagard, Norman **9**:44
Thames, Battle of the **2**:73; **3**:29
Thanksgiving **1**:47; **4**:5
"That's one small step for a man, one giant leap for mankind" **8**:55
Thaw, Harry K. **5**:57
theater
  Death of a Salesman **7**:72
  Ford's Theatre **4**:31
  Great Gatsby, The **6**:39
  see also musical theater
Thomas, Charles **9**:70
Thomas, George Henry **4**:14
Thomas, Henry **8**:95
Thomas, Lowell **6**:35
Thomas, Robert Bailey **2**:42
Thomas Flyer (automobile) **5**:62
Thompson, Fred **9**:77
Thomson, Bobby **7**:80
Thoreau, Henry David **3**:43
Thorpe, Jim **5**:74
3-D movies **7**:82
Three Mile Island accident **8**:86
Thunderbird (automobile) **7**:88
Thurmond, Strom **7**:66
Ticonderoga, Fort **1**:96; **2**:6
Tilden, Bill **4**:60
Tilden, Samuel J. **4**:62, 66, 67
Time (magazine) **6**:32; **9**:94
Times Square (New York City) **9**:95
Tinian **7**:37, 63
Tippecanoe, Battle of **2**:69; **3**:29
"Tippecanoe and Tyler too" **2**:69; **3**:29
tires, rationing of **6**:90; **7**:16
TIROS I **8**:10
Titanic (movie) **9**:86
Titanic (ship) **5**:74, 75, 93
Tituba **1**:61
Titusville (Pennsylvania) **3**:75
tobacco plantations **2**:60
Todd house **2**:9
Tokyo (Japan), Doolittle's raid on **7**:7
Tomahawk missiles **9**:64
Tom Thumb (steam locomotive) **3**:9
Tonquin (ship) **2**:68
Toomer, Jean **6**:36
Torah **1**:78

Torch, Operation **7**:14
Torgau (Germany) **7**:50
tornadoes **9**:94
tourism **5**:93, 94; **6**:53
  see also national parks
Touro, Isaac **1**:78
Touro Synagogue **1**:78
Townshend Acts **1**:79
toys and games
  Barbie dolls **8**:7
  bridge **6**:63
  Hula-Hoops **7**:96
  mah-jongg **6**:28
  teddy bears **5**:45
trade
  clipper ships **3**:51
  Gray, Robert **2**:43
  Japan, opening of **2**:72; **3**:65
  St. Lawrence Seaway **8**:5
  Santa Fe Trail **2**:83
  triangular slave trade **1**:64
  see also interstate commerce
Trail of Tears **1**:10; **3**:24
trains, railroad *see* railroads
Trans-Alaska Pipeline **8**:72, 82
transcontinental railroad **4**:46, 79
transistors **7**:69
transportation
  bicycles **5**:19
  covered wagons **3**:34
  Erie Canal **2**:91
  Holland Tunnel **6**:47
  Lunar Roving Vehicle **8**:64
  Panama Canal **5**:86
  Sherman tanks **7**:8
  stagecoaches **2**:85
  subways **5**:17
  trolley cars **4**:78
  see also automobiles; aviation; boats and boating; railroads; ships and shipping
travel *see* tourism
Travis, William B. **3**:17
Travolta, John **8**:79
Trent (ship) **3**:25
Trenton (New Jersey) **2**:14
Trenton, Battle of **2**:5, 15, 16
Triangle fire **5**:70, 71
triangular slave trade **1**:64
triodes **5**:69
Tripoli **2**:57
trolley cars **4**:78
Truman, Harry S. **7**:44, 45, 65, 73, 76, 81; **8**:66
  atomic bomb **7**:54
  desegregation of armed forces **7**:9, 67; **9**:87
  election of 1948 **7**:66
  Korean War **7**:74
  MacArthur, Douglas **7**:77
  Marshall Plan **7**:68
  Medicare and Medicaid **8**:40
  Potsdam Conference **7**:53
  Young, Solomon **2**:83
Trumbull, John **1**:92
trust-busting **4**:95; **5**:45
Truth, Sojourner **3**:62
Tubman, Harriet **3**:21
Tunisia **7**:14, 24
tunnels **6**:47
Tunney, Gene **6**:44
Turner, Nat **3**:11
Tuskegee airmen **7**:9
Tutuila **5**:39
TV dinners **7**:70
Twain, Mark **2**:93; **3**:76; **4**:59, 83
Tweed, "Boss" **4**:54
Twentieth Century Limited (train) **5**:94
Twenty-One **8**:6
Tyler, A. **5**:21
Tyler, John **2**:69; **3**:29, 30, 35
typesetting **4**:81
typewriters **4**:59
typhoid fever **5**:34
Tyson, Cicely **8**:81

U

U-2 incident **8**:12
UFOs **9**:78
Uggams, Leslie **8**:81
Ulion, Gretchen **9**:88
Unabomber suspect, arrest of **9**:56
Uncle Sam **2**:77; **5**:9
Uncle Tom's Cabin **3**:62
undercover operations **9**:12
Underground Railroad **3**:13, 21
unemployment **5**:9, 15; **6**:50, 67, 75
Union of Soviet Socialist Republics **8**:21, 66; **9**:21
  Apollo-Soyuz Test Project **8**:76
  Cuban missile crisis **8**:25
  Olympic Games (1980) **8**:88
  Potsdam Conference **7**:53
  Sputnik I **7**:92
  U-2 incident **8**:12
  U.S. and Soviet troops meet at Elbe River **7**:50
  Yalta Conference **7**:46
  see also Cold War
Union Pacific Railroad **4**:46, 56
Unisys **5**:11
United Nations **7**:44, 55
  Albright, Madeleine **9**:71
  Atlantic Charter **6**:92
  Bush, George **9**:16
  Fourth World Conference on Women **9**:47
  Iraq crisis (1997–1998) **9**:90
  John Paul II's 1995 visit to U.S. **9**:49
  Somalia, American troops in **9**:27
  Yalta Conference **7**:46
United States (ship) **5**:93
UNIVAC **7**:59, 76
universities *see* colleges and universities
uranium **6**:54; **7**:15
Utah **3**:48; **4**:46
Utopian communities **2**:92

V

vaccination, polio **7**:83
Valentine's Day Massacre **6**:56
Valley Forge **2**:16, 21
Valley Forge National Historical Park **2**:20
Van Buren, Martin **3**:16, 22
Vance, Vivian **7**:79
Vanderbilt, Alva **4**:79
Vanderbilt, Harold **6**:63
Vanderbilt, William K. **4**:79
Van Doren, Charles **8**:6
Veracruz (Mexico) **5**:85
Vereen, Ben **8**:81
Vermont **1**:96; **2**:16, 65; **4**:13
Verrazano, Giovanni da **1**:20
Verrazano-Narrows Bridge **1**:20
Vesey conspiracy **2**:84
Vespucci, Amerigo **1**:18
veterans **6**:51, 61; **7**:33, 43, 62
vice presidents of the United States
  Ferraro's nomination **9**:9
  see also names of vice presidents
Vichy government (France) **7**:14
Vicksburg, Siege of **4**:5, 9
victory gardens **7**:18
Vietnam War **8**:47, 53, 66, 69
  Cambodia, invasion of **8**:60
  DaNang, landing at **8**:38
  demonstrations against **8**:44, 59
  Ford, Gerald R. **8**:74
  Johnson, Lyndon Baines **8**:32
  Kent State killings **8**:62
  Nixon, Richard M. **8**:54
  Pentagon Papers **8**:63
  Strategic Air Command **7**:58
  U.S. withdrawal **8**:70
  Vietnam Veterans Memorial **8**:96
  Westmoreland, William **8**:48
Viking Mars probes **8**:77, 78
Vikings **1**:12

Villa, Pancho **5**:90
Vincennes (ship) **3**:25
Vinland **1**:12
Virginia
  1619 **1**:42
  1692 **1**:61
  Appomattox Court House National Historical Park **4**:29
  Bacon's Rebellion **1**:55, 56
  Bull Run, First Battle of **3**:85
  Bull Run, Second Battle of **3**:90
  Chancellorsville, Battle of **4**:8
  first captive Africans **1**:43
  Fredericksburg, Battle of **3**:95
  Gosnold, Bartholomew **1**:35
  Jamestown, founding of **1**:37
  Jamestown Festival Park **1**:39
  Jefferson, Thomas **2**:56
  Manassas National Battlefield Park **3**:91
  Monroe, James **2**:78
  Monticello **1**:83
  Mosby's Rangers **4**:17
  Mount Vernon **1**:75
  Peninsular Campaign **3**:88
  Petersburg, Siege of **4**:22
  plantations **2**:60
  Shenandoah Valley campaign **4**:25
  Spotsylvania, Battle of **4**:21
  tornadoes (1998) **9**:94
  Turner's rebellion **3**:11
  Wilder, Douglas **9**:15
  Wilderness, Battle of the **4**:20
  William and Mary, College of **1**:63
  Williamsburg **1**:50
  Yorktown, British surrender at **2**:28
Virginia (warship) *see* Merrimack
Virginia City (Nevada) **3**:76
Virginia Company **1**:38, 42
Virgin Islands, U.S. **5**:92, 96
Vladivostok (Russia) **6**:11
volcanoes **1**:8; **8**:88
volleyball **3**:60
volunteerism **8**:17; **9**:75
voting *see* suffrage
Voting Rights Act of 1965 **8**:37
vulcanized rubber **3**:27

W

Waco raid **9**:30
wagon trains *see* covered wagons
Wake Island **6**:91
Waldseemüller, Martin **1**:18
Walesa, Lech **9**:19
Walker, James **4**:14
Walker, Mary **4**:7
Wallace, George **8**:37, 66
Wallace, Henry **7**:66
Wallace, Mike **8**:51
Walt Disney Company **9**:45
Wampanoag Indians **1**:46, 47, 55, 58
Wanamaker, John **4**:44
War, Secretary of **5**:63
war brides **7**:56
war crimes **4**:19; **7**:57
Warhol, Andy **8**:26
Warm Springs (Georgia) **7**:49
War of 1812 **2**:70, 71, 74
  Erie, Lake, Battle of **2**:72
  Florida **2**:82
  Fort Astoria **2**:68
  Harrison, William Henry **3**:29
  Horseshoe Bend **2**:75
  Jackson, Andrew **3**:6
  Library of Congress **2**:54
  Madison, James **2**:67
  Navy, United States **2**:46
  New Orleans, Battle of **2**:76
  Ojibwe (Chippewa) **1**:73
  "Old Ironsides" **2**:50; **9**:81
  Pike, Zebulon **2**:64
  Taylor, Zachary **3**:56
  Thames, Battle of the **2**:73
  Uncle Sam **2**:77

War of 1812 (cont.)
  Washington (D.C.) **2:**52
  White House **2:**53
Warren, Earl **7:**87; **8:**35
Warren Commission Report **8:**35
Warsaw Pact **7:**71
Washington (D.C.)
  1793 **2:**45
  Bicentennial (U.S.) **8:**77
  civil-rights march (1963) **6:**31;
    8:31
  Ford's Theatre **4:**31
  Library of Congress **2:**54
  Lincoln Memorial **6:**31
  "Million Man March" **9:**50
  national capital **2:**52
  Promise Keepers rally **9:**82
  Smithsonian Institution **3:**45
  Vietnam Veterans Memorial
    8:96
  War of 1812 **2:**71, 74
  Washington Monument **4:**82
  Watergate scandal **8:**67
  White House **2:**53
Washington (state) **2:**43; **5:**26; **6:**94;
    8:88
Washington, George **1:**74, 88; **2:**5,
    16, 21, 25, 38, 45
  Adams, John **2:**49
  cannon of Ticonderoga **2:**6
  Constitution, ratification of the
    2:35
  Constitutional Convention **2:**33
  Continental Congress, First
    1:87
  crosses the Delaware **2:**14
  declined to seek third term **6:**88
  former general elected
    president **9:**46
  French and Indian War **1:**72
  Harpers Ferry **3:**74
  inauguration **2:**37
  Long Island, Battle of **2:**10
  Monmouth, Battle of **2:**23
  Mount Rushmore **6:**93
  Mount Vernon **1:**75
  Princeton, Battle of **2:**17
  Second Continental Congress
    1:93
  Touro Synagogue **1:**78
  Trenton, Battle of **2:**15
  Valley Forge **2:**20
  Washington (D.C.) **2:**52
  Washington Monument **4:**82
  Whiskey Rebellion **2:**47
  White House, never lived in
    2:53
  White Plains, Battle of **2:**13
  Yorktown, British surrender at
    2:28
Washington, Mount, cog railway **4:**49
Washington Monument **3:**56; **4:**82
Washington Post **8:**63, 69, 73
Washoe Valley **3:**76
Watergate scandal **8:**54, 66, 67, 69,
    73
Watson, George **9:**70
Watson Brake Mounds **1:**5
Wayne, John **5:**79
Waynesborough, Battle of **4:**25
wealth **2:**68; **4:**79
weather **2:**42; **9:**67, 93, 94
weather satellites **8:**10
Webster, Daniel **3:**62; **5:**12
Webster, Noah **2:**95
"We have met the enemy, and they
    are ours" **2:**72
welfare *see* social welfare
Welland Canal **8:**5
Welles, Orson **6:**95
Wells, Horace **3:**31
Welsh, Joseph **7:**86
West, Benjamin **2:**29
West, The
  covered wagons **3:**34
  cowboys and cattle drives **4:**37
  Harrison, William Henry **3:**29
  mountain men **2:**86

Pike, Zebulon **2:**64
Smith, Jedediah **2:**87
  see also outlaws; pioneer life
Westinghouse, George **4:**51
Westinghouse Electric Corporation
    4:51; **9:**45
Westmoreland, William **8:**48
West Point (New York) **2:**58
West Virginia **3:**74; **4:**77
whaling **2:**96; **3:**61
Wham-O (company) **7:**96
"What hath God wrought!" **3:**37
Whigs **3:**30, 56
Whiskey Rebellion **2:**47
White, Edward H., II **8:**36, 39, 45
White, Elijah **3:**33
White, John **1:**33, 34
White, Pearl **5:**79
White, Stanford, murder of **5:**57
White House **2:**49, 52, 53, 74; **9:**77
White Plains, Battle of **2:**13
Whitewater affair **9:**96
Whitfield, George **1:**67
Whitney, Eli **2:**45, 48
Whyte, Sandra **9:**88
wildcatters **5:**44
Wilder, Douglas **9:**15
Wilderness, Battle of the **4:**20
Wilderness Trail **1:**88
wildlife **9:**15, 17
Wiley, Harvey W. **5:**56
Wilkes, Charles **3:**25
Wilkes expedition **3:**25
William and Mary, College of **1:**63
William Johnson House **3:**40
Williams, Daniel Hale **5:**9
Williams, Ted **6:**90
Williamsburg (Virginia) **1:**50, 63
Willkie, Wendell **6:**88
Wills, Helen **4:**60
Willys-Overland Motors, Inc. **7:**28
Wilmington (Delaware) **1:**48
Wilson, Sam **2:**77
Wilson, Woodrow **5:**74, 81, 85, 92;
    6:5, 21
  election of 1912 **5:**76
  Fourteen Points **6:**15
  Lusitania, sinking of the **5:**89
  Pershing, John J. **5:**90
  Virgin Islands, U.S. **5:**96
  Zimmermann Telegram **5:**95
Winchester, Battle of **4:**25
Winchester rifle **4:**50
Winslet, Kate **9:**86
Winthrop, John **1:**49
Wirz, Henry **4:**19
Wisconsin **1:**52; **2:**36, 89; **3:**12; **4:**54
witch-hunt, Salem **1:**61, 62
"With malice toward none, with
    charity for all..." **4:**27
Wizard of Oz, The **6:**85
woman suffrage **3:**52; **4:**48; **6:**21,
    24, 25
women
  1942 **7:**5
  Albright, Madeleine **9:**71
  bicycles **5:**19
  Borden, Lizzie **5:**13
  Coast Guard, U.S. **2:**40
  Earhart, Amelia **6:**80
  Ferraro, Geraldine **9:**9
  flappers **6:**82
  Girl Scouts **5:**77
  Godey's Lady's Book **3:**10
  Lipinski, Tara **9:**89
  Lowell textile mills **3:**19
  McDaniel, Hattie **6:**87
  Miss America Pageant **6:**26
  Oberlin College admits women
    3:13
  O'Connor, Sandra Day **8:**91
  Parks, Rosa **7:**89
  Perkins, Frances **6:**67
  Rosie the Riveter **7:**17
  Sacagawea **2:**62
  Seneca Falls Convention **3:**52
  suffrage **6:**21, 24, 25

U.S. ice-hockey team wins
    Olympic gold medal **9:**88
  war brides **7:**56
  West Point **2:**58
  Women's Army Corps **7:**22
  Yale University **1:**65
Women's Army Corps (WAC) **7:**5, 22
women's rights **3:**52, 53; **4:**48; **9:**47
  see also woman suffrage
Wood, Leonard **5:**33
Woods, Tiger **9:**68
Woodstock Festival **8:**53, 57
Woodward, Bob **8:**69
Woolworth, F.W. **4:**44; **9:**80
Wooster (Ohio) **4:**13
Worcester (Massachusetts) **6:**24
Works Progress Administration *see*
    WPA
World's Columbian Exposition **5:**10,
    14
World Series **3:**42; **6:**18, 32; **9:**15
World's Fair (1939) **5:**47
World Trade Center bombing **9:**29
World War I **5:**85, 92; **6:**5
  Belleau Wood, Battle of **6:**10
  Cantigny, Battle of **6:**8
  Château-Thierry, Battle of **6:**9
  Curtiss, Glenn **5:**73
  Girl Scouts' peach-pit drive **5:**77
  Johnson, Henry **6:**7
  Lafayette Escadrille **5:**91
  Liberty bonds **6:**6
  Lusitania, sinking of the **5:**89
  Marne, Second Battle of the
    6:12
  Meuse-Argonne offensive **6:**14
  military aviation **7:**61
  St. Mihiel, Battle of **6:**13
  submarines **5:**38
  U.S. troops in Russia **6:**11
  veterans in Bonus Army **6:**61
  Wilson, Woodrow **5:**81
  Wilson's Fourteen Points **6:**15
  Zimmermann Telegram **5:**95
World War II **6:**85, 90; **7:**5, 21, 33,
    44
  African-American veterans
    receive Medal of Honor
    9:70
  aircraft carriers **7:**13
  Air Force, U.S. **7:**61
  Allies cross the Rhine **7:**48
  Anzio, invasion at **7:**35
  Atlantic Charter **6:**92
  atomic bombs **7:**52, 54
  B-17 "Flying Fortress" **7:**23
  Bataan **7:**6
  Bulge, Battle of the **7:**42
  Bush, George **9:**16
  Casablanca **7:**19
  Code Talkers **7:**10
  Coral Sea, Battle of the **7:**11
  D-Day **7:**38
  Doolittle's raid on Tokyo **7:**7
  early radio **6:**35
  Eisenhower, Dwight D. **7:**84
  experimental jet fighters **8:**8
  50th anniversary of war's end
    9:48
  442nd Regimental Combat
    Team **7:**27
  "Geronimo" used as battle cry
    4:87
  Gilbert Islands, Battle of the
    7:31
  Guadalcanal, Battle of **7:**30
  Guam **5:**36
  Italy, invasion of **7:**26
  Iwo Jima, Battle of **7:**47
  Japanese-Americans,
    internment of **7:**20
  Jeeps **7:**28
  Kasserine Pass, Battle of the
    7:24
  Leyte Gulf, Battle of **7:**41
  Mariana Islands, Battles of **7:**37

Market-Garden, Operation **7:**40
  Marshall Islands, Battle of the
    7:34
  Midway, Battle of **7:**12
  Miller, Glenn **6:**76
  Monte Cassino, Battles for **7:**36
  Navy, United States **2:**46
  North Africa, invasion of **7:**14
  Northern Mariana Islands **7:**63
  Nuremberg trials **7:**57
  ocean liners **5:**93
  Okinawa, Battle of **7:**51
  Paris, liberation of **7:**39
  Pearl Harbor **6:**96
  Potsdam Conference **7:**53
  rationing **7:**16
  Roosevelt, Franklin D. **6:**68
  Rosie the Riveter **7:**17
  segregation in the armed forces
    7:67
  Selective Service Act **6:**89
  Sherman tanks **7:**8
  Sicily, invasion of **7:**25
  Solomon Islands, Battle of the
    7:29
  Truman, Harry S. **7:**45
  Tuskegee airmen **7:**9
  U.S. and Soviet troops meet at
    Elbe River **7:**50
  U.S.–Japan peace treaty (1951)
    7:76
  victory gardens **7:**18
  Wake Island **6:**91
  war brides **7:**56
  Westmoreland, William **8:**48
  Women's Army Corps **7:**22
  Yalta Conference **7:**46
WORM drives **8:**83
Wounded Knee, Battle of **4:**95, 96
WPA (Works Progress
    Administration) **6:**73, 78
Wright, Orville and Wilbur **5:**49, 73;
    7:61
Wrigley Company **5:**85
Wupatki National Monument **1:**8
Wyle, Noah **9:**36
Wyoming **4:**48, 55; **6:**34

X-Y-Z

Xerox Corporation **6:**84
Yale University **1:**65; **5:**5, 63
Yalta Conference **7:**44, 46
Yamato (Japanese battleship) **7:**51
"Yankee" (nickname) **2:**44
Yankee Clipper (airplane) **6:**77
Yankee clippers **3:**51
"Yankee Doodle" **1:**74
Yankee peddlers **2:**44
Yeager, Chuck **7:**61; **9:**83
"years to remember" *see* index
    section preceding the A's
yellow fever **2:**52; **5:**28, 34
Yellow Kid **5:**18
Yellowstone National Park **4:**55; **9:**14
Yeltsin, Boris **9:**48
YMCA **3:**60
Yorktown (aircraft carrier) **7:**12
Yorktown, Battle of **2:**25, 28, 38
Yosemite National Park **4:**95
"You may fire when you are ready,
    Gridley" **5:**30
Young, Brigham **3:**36, 48
Young, Cy **5:**51
Young, John **8:**94
Young, Solomon **2:**83
Young Men's Christian Association
    see YMCA
young people *see* children
Youth's Companion, The **5:**7
Zenger, John Peter **1:**71
Ziegfeld, Florenz **5:**59
Ziegfeld Follies **5:**59
Zimmermann, Arthur **5:**95
Zimmermann Telegram **5:**95
zippers **5:**14
Zunis **1:**21, 22, 23